Remembered Voices

Remembered Voices

Reclaiming the Legacy of "Neo-Orthodoxy"

Douglas John Hall

Westminster John Knox Press
Louisville, Kentucky

Grateful acknowledgment is made to SCM Press, London,
and Westminster John Knox Press for permission to
reproduce material from Emil Brunner, *The Divine-
Human Encounter* (Philadelphia and London, 1943–44).

Book design by Sharon Adams
Cover design by Pam Poll

First edition
Published by Westminster John Knox Press
Louisville, Kentucky

This book is printed on acid-free paper that meets the
American National Standards Institute Z39.48 standard. ♾

PRINTED IN THE UNITED STATES OF AMERICA
98 99 00 01 02 03 04 05 06 07 — 10 9 8 7 6 5 4 3 2 1

Library of Congress Cataloging-in-Publication Data

Hall, Douglas John, 1928–
    Remembered voices : reclaiming the legacy of "neo-
orthodoxy" / Douglas John Hall. — 1st ed.
        p.   cm.
    Includes bibliographical references and index.
    ISBN 0-664-25772-0 (alk. paper)
    1. Neo-orthodoxy.   I. Title.
BT83.2.H35   1998
230'.046—dc21   98-34782

For Rhoda

Contents

Preface

As the twentieth century draws to a close, and with it my own professional career, I have felt strongly the need to recall the theological renewal that attended both the century's and my own beginnings. How should one view, from the perspective of what has happened since and what appears on the near horizon, that great renovation of Christian thought, faith, and life?

For me, as for many of my contemporaries, this cannot be a merely academic exercise, another investigation of twentieth-century Christian theology. Whether we have found our life's work in theology, biblical studies, historical studies, or other fields of Christian scholarship, or in the parish ministry, or along quite different vocational lines, we have been profoundly shaped by the great themes and concerns of that movement. Our lives, not only our ideas and our work, are necessarily involved in any such retrospective.

The impact of teachers like Reinhold Niebuhr, Paul Tillich, Wilhelm Pauck, and so many others who were (I would say providentially!) assembled at Union Theological Seminary in the 1950s is not something that one forgets or outlives. I do not think that I have been unduly dependent on any of these teachers, or on the others who were part of that international community of Christian scholarship. It has certainly not been my intention to imitate all or any of them. But I know that I have been deeply influenced by their work, and that, collectively, they still define for me the criteria, not only of what "excellence" in theology would have to mean but—more importantly—the meaning of Christ's discipleship.

The overall conclusion that I have reached in this act of recall is contained, *in nuce,* in the subtitle of the book: there is, I think, a rich legacy here that has not been adequately appropriated. And I believe that the future of Protestantism in North America depends upon whether and to what extent that heritage is laid hold of, both by Christian scholars and the churches, in the years and decades ahead.

That thesis was first explored in the Currie Lectures, given at Austin Presbyterian Theological Seminary in January 1995. Four of the seven chapters of this book (those on Barth, Tillich, Reinhold Niebuhr, and Bonhoeffer) were first presented as lectures in that context. I have altered them somewhat to conform to their presentation as chapters in this book, but I have wished to retain, at the same time, their character both as address and as personal testimony. The same spirit, to a lesser extent, informs the three subsequently written chapters as well as the Introduction and the Conclusions.

I am grateful to the sponsors of the Currie Lectureship and to the faculty and student body of Austin Theological Seminary for the invitation to participate in this well-known lecture series, and I should like to express my thanks to those who made my and my wife's stay in Dallas and Austin so very pleasant.

Douglas John Hall

Notre-Dame-de-Grâce,
Montréal, Québec, Canada
Winter 1998

Introduction

When at the age of sixty-two Karl Barth penned the second of his three successive "How I Changed My Mind" articles for the *Christian Century,* he noted that in the decade from 1938 to 1948 he had been sufficiently occupied with "the demands of life and vocation" to keep the door closed, "at least partly, to backward-looking self-contemplation, that weakness of age."[1] Ten years later, Barth's rather austere assessment of the retrospections of age had given way to an opinion that, having myself come closer to Barth's then-seventy-two years, I find more to my liking. In his report on the decade 1948–1958, after acknowledging the "notorious fact that [he had] become an old man," the famous theologian of Basel wrote:

> Along with an increasing comprehension of the historicity of all human nature and of my own existence, I have learned to become more attentive to, more lovingly conscious of, my connections with my forebears and at the same time to participate more and more in the lives of my children and of my children's children.[2]

This statement, if it is understood (as it should be) to imply a transpersonal reference, expresses very well the perspective that I wish to bring to this small study. The seven chapters will concern some of my own "forebears"—not, of course, in the biological but certainly in the intellectual and spiritual sense. Two of them, Reinhold Niebuhr and Paul Tillich, were for several years my teachers; the others, through their published works (and, in the cases of H. Richard Niebuhr and Karl Barth, occasional lectures in person), taught me from afar. And while I have always been conscious of the formative influence of these thinkers upon my life and work, I would at this transition point in my life gladly acknowledge, with Barth, that the "increasing comprehension of the historicity of all human nature and of my own existence" that comes with age has made me "more attentive to, more lovingly conscious of, my connection with [these and other] forebears."

Historical consciousness of the most existential sort is perhaps reserved for one's latter years. By seventy, one has begun to reckon with the inexorable fact that one is not immortal. It can be a rather daunting—even a melancholy—experience. But such melancholy, which Albrecht Dürer in his well-known etching *Melancholia* wisely associated with the swift and irreversible passage of time, is wonderfully chastened by the recall of those who have gone before, who have faced the known and the unknown with courage and imagination, and who have left us with a rich legacy of wisdom as a guide for our own journey. In the field of Christian theology, and in the Christian community at large, I feel we can be grateful that those who have been our twentieth-century forebears in this tradition and vocation have been persons upon whose insight we can still draw without embarrassment.

But I do not intend these reflections as eulogies, nor as exercises in nostalgia, and therefore the second part of the aging Barth's confession concerning the consequences of his heightened historical consciousness—involvement in the struggles of present and future generations—must also be emphasized. There is, of course, a kind of "backward-looking self-contemplation" that must indeed be considered a *"weakness* of age." But many of us who are older are granted the special grace of participating quite fully, through our involvement with our children and grandchildren, our students, or the younger cohorts of society and church, in the present and impending future. And the question that is then put to us, as bridge figures between the past and the future, is not just whether we remember but whether and to what extent we can bring forth from memory the stuff out of which hope is made. The authenticating test of the remembrance of things past is its capacity to help decipher the always-indistinct present and to point a way into the future. Every Eucharist reminds or ought to remind us of that.

Today, abandoned to a fragmented and bewildering present, the church's need for such remembering is, I think, greater than ever. Far from being an exercise in autobiographic reflection on the part of an individual on the verge of his own transition to "the biblical age," therefore, these reflections on some of the great mentors of the Christian movement during the first part of the present century have been undertaken in the consciousness that Christianity itself is undergoing an immense transition—a veritable metamorphosis, as I have argued heretofore.[3] Standing at the threshold of a millennium reckoned as third on the basis of the chronology of the triumphant "Christian" West, we are confronted by a vastly altered world situation, a global marketplace in which the concept of an all-conquering Christendom can have no place. Yet sixteen centuries of imperial Christianity have conditioned Christians to expect an ever-ascending sojourn through time and, consequently, to be rendered despondent and perplexed, often, at the prospect of a less auspicious future.

Our discomfiture as Christians and churchfolk in the face of the present ecclesiastical metamorphosis—a discomfiture increasingly evident at the quantitative as well as the qualitative levels of measurement—is reflected more subtly in the generally "deconstructive" mood of the most popular contemporary theological movements and offerings. So much of what today's scholars remember of this tradition seems to be in need of revision—much of it, apparently, of outright rejection!

I share with such interpreters the belief that responsible Christian thought today, as always, must submit what has been handed over to us from the past to careful and unsentimental scrutiny. Not only must it be tested for its open or subtle support of oppressive attitudes and demeaning practices; it must be examined in the light of the judgment of Christian hubris that is surely "judgment beginning at the household of faith." In what we have received, in what we ourselves often still naively promulgate, there are assumptions about the mission and destiny of the Christian religion that will not and should not stand in the face of Christendom's "humiliation" (Albert van den Heuvel)—a humiliation that I take to be providential. The critical theologies that characterize the last three or four decades of the century have been, it seems to me, a necessary prelude to any conceivable reconstruction of the faith that would be wise enough to help Christianity move into the future both faithfully in relation to the tradition and responsibly in relation to the life of our beleaguered planet.

It is toward reconstruction, however, that we must certainly move, and it is my conviction that the seven thinkers whom I shall discuss here, along with many others belonging to the theological movement labeled "neo-orthodoxy," can aid us in this transition to theological rebuilding in ways that many if not most contemporary Christian scholars fail to recognize. The deconstructive approach has, I feel, been so consistently applied also to these representatives of our immediate past that we have neglected to discern some of the positive ways in which they already both anticipated our struggle and provided guidelines for our enterprise. Perhaps we have been so preoccupied with their errors and omissions (their abiding sexism and androcentrism, their Eurocentrism, their Christomonism, and the like) that we are unable to perceive the deeper relevance of their work for today.

One does not, of course, suggest that these thinkers have been written off. Only the most extreme dismissers of the Christian past would propose such a thing. They are all "remembered voices"— in places beloved, here and there (alas!) idolized. But I think they can be of greater use to us if we pay stricter attention to their own words and less—much less—to the images, typologies, and reputations that have been spun around their names, whether by their critics or their more zealous and promotional admirers. The contribution to Christian self-understanding that the movement called "neo-orthodoxy" has to offer those who continue to study the writings of its greatest exponents represents, after all, one of the richest, most encyclopedic outpourings of Christian theological work in the entire history of this faith. And there are emphases, insights, nuances, turnings, and directives—"legacies"—within this great opus that have never been properly claimed and deployed. Their voices are remembered—how could it be otherwise? But many of their words have been neglected, unheard, or plainly forgotten. And that is unfortunate, because we need those words—more, even, than did their contemporaries.

It is certainly not my aim to explore all that these forebears have to teach us. It would be ridiculous to attempt anything like a survey of their thought in such a slim volume. I intend, rather, to choose, in the case of each subject, *one major point of concentration*. My choice will not, I hope, be thought purely arbitrary. Throughout, I wish to consider these reflections on our theological predecessors primarily as one returning to them for guidance—not, then, in the spirit of a remembering that seeks refuge in the past but of that recall which, touched by divine grace, may really become productive of hope.

One term in the subtitle of this book demands particular explanation: "neo-orthodoxy." That term has been placed in quotes because, by all standards of investigation, it is a highly ambiguous term *and always has been*. As H. Martin Rumscheidt writes, "The term, invented by critics, was never quite free of denigrative connotation."[4] John Godsey, in his article for the *Encyclopedia of Religion*,[5] notes that this nomenclature is "used mainly in the English-speaking world," and he suggests that "the neorthodox [*sic*] movement could more accurately be called neo-Reformation theology." Another commentator (rather insightfully, it seems to me) writes that "The term is generally used by those who would not identify themselves with such a theology, either because it seems to deviate too much from the orthodoxy of the Reformation theologians and classical Protestant confessions of faith, or because it is too narrowly orthodox."[6] Still another author, aiming beyond definition of the term itself to what, in his view, it stands for, doubts that even moderates found this movement acceptable: "Neo-orthodoxy's stance toward the conservatives and the liberals has satisfied neither group, and the moderates have not embraced it. Thus," he concludes condescendingly, "although one cannot ignore the movement, its ultimate place in the history of theology is not yet clear."[7]

Undoubtedly it betrays a certain Kierkegaardian contrariety, but I cannot suppress my satisfaction at the manner in which this movement of theological renewal still defies categorization. Not only "neo-orthodoxy," but none of the other terms that are sometimes applied to it ("theology of crisis," "dialectical theology," even "neo-Reformation" theology) are really acceptable. Happily so! For whenever such lively phenomena are named, they too easily fall prey to intellectual and spiritual immunity: they can be embraced or dismissed without much ado, the label alone sufficing to determine their content and significance.

Those who have actually lived with the thought of the authors associated with this movement know that, whatever else may be said of it, "neo-orthodoxy" *was* a lively phenomenon; only the uninformed can approach it with condescension or indifference. Whether one confines the movement to those clustered around Karl Barth, which seems to be a very narrow circumscription,[8] or considers it expansively enough to include the Niebuhrs, Tillich, Bultmann,[9] and others who were critical of Barth, as I do,[10] one cannot miss or dismiss the fact that this "new theology," by whatever name, *was new*—was and became, in fact, the cutting edge of Christian thought throughout the first half of this century—or more accurately let us say from about 1910 to 1960, fifty years. As for the nomenclature, every one of the persons associated with this movement whether vigorously or nonchalantly, rejected the term "neo-orthodoxy." And part of their reason for doing so—a rather large part, in fact—was because, as representatives of positions that were as critical of reactionary orthodoxy as they were of the reigning liberalism, they resented the dismissal of their witness which put it down to a mere return to past theological conventions and biases.

What, then, does constitute this movement? Is there anything binding these many and diverse figures together—supposing that we agree upon the broader understanding of who may be said to have participated in this movement?

I shall reserve for my Conclusions the fuller answer that I wish to give to this question. I do so for two reasons: first, because it can only be a meaningful answer if it follows an investigation, however brief, of some of the thinkers in question; second, and more importantly, because one's response to such a historical inquiry depends on the perspective from which one views the past, and that perspective is itself (unless it has been framed and fixed to serve some extraneous need!) a moving, changing thing. It may be true that the past is unchangeable: as the late George P. Grant was wont to say, what has been *has been*. But the *meaning* of the past is not fixed. In one's search for bearings amid the "ever-rolling stream" of time, the past is a rich resource of experience that offers one ever-new treasures, accommodating itself graciously enough to one's present needs without divulging its entire mystery and meaning.

I can best illustrate my meaning here from my own history of involvement with the theological movement under discussion. It was my experience as a student of these forebears that one could (most of us in fact did) sympathize so strongly with one or another of these great thinkers, or with an identifiable school among them, that the others seemed decisively, irretrievably "other." When, however, I had to assume the role of a teaching theologian myself; when I left the enchanting but always rather hypothetical world of the graduate school and encountered, without much insulation, that of the all-too-empirical church and its host society; when I came up against the religious and doctrinal positions actually and noisily dominant within that sphere; when I underwent, with everyone else, the subsequent religious enthusiasms and trends, with one "theology of" following hard on the heels of the other, I began gradually to realize that positions I had once regarded as incompatible were in reality far closer than I had thought. From the perspective of 1998, the theological debates of 1948 (and ten or fifteen years on either side of that year) assume a quite different character. Hindsight, given all that has happened between the times, makes Barth, Tillich, and Reinhold Niebuhr (to name only three) far more collegial than they themselves, perhaps, could have realized—just as it makes Luther, Calvin, and Zwingli, for all their famous differences, members of a movement we all without hesitation call " the Reformation." Individual differences are not lost sight of, but they can be contained, without doing them injustice, in a larger dialogue and process whose essential integrity is made plainer by subsequent history.

One could, of course, attribute the degree of commonality among these thinkers to their shared historical context. It was after all a highly evocative context for sensitive Christians. Both modernity, with which the mentors of these theologians had so steadfastly attempted a concordat, and Christendom itself were beginning conspicuously to break down. It is not accidental that while the theological debates and the manifestos of this movement cannot be called apocalyptic, they are nevertheless permeated by the sense of an ending. All of the scholars in question are responding to immense and unsettling questions posed for Western civilization, and for humanity at large, by the momentous and often terrifying events of the epoch. These questions predate "the guns of August" (1914) by which they are first and most unmistakably punctuated, and they persist and multiply well beyond "the Great War." Indeed, as the much-heralded twentieth-century (the *Christian* century!) progresses, it proves to be a century filled with unending and complexly interwoven questions, questions undreamed-of, at least, by this generation of theologians, schooled as they all were in the optimistic credo of liberal Christianity, and unprepared for the revelation that Christianity itself was implicated in the terrible decline and decay they witnessed. Was theirs not, therefore, more a solidarity of questions than of answers?

Perhaps. Certainly these theologians are more conspicuously at one in their sense of what is wrong with their world than they are in proposing how the wrong might be righted. Perhaps movements are usually defined more obviously by what their adherents fear and reject than by what they wish to achieve or preserve. Yet, even in their analyses of "the situation," to use Tillich's familiar category, there are shared assumptions throughout the literary testimonies of these authors—assumptions that are not shared, concepts that are not explored, by non-Christian cartographers of their world; for instance, despite its relegation by liberalism to the theological dark ages, all of these authors seem spontaneously moved to restore and revamp the ancient language of "sin"—even of "*original* sin."

But beyond such recourse to jettisoned or almost-discarded symbolic language in their attempts to discern and name the darker signs of their times, these theologians manifest certain common presuppositions and intentions also when they attempt to reformulate the faith constructively. The unanimity (not uniformity!) of their positive Christian witness becomes more transparent against the backdrop of the more recent and contemporary theological dialogue. And it meets us, not as mere historical theology, but as a prophetic summons. Throughout these chapters implicitly, and explicitly in the Conclusions, I shall argue that, taken as a whole, "neo-orthodoxy" issues a challenge that, as it moves into the twenty-first century, Christianity in general and Protestantism in particular dare not ignore. It may even be necessary, in the process, to find some way of redeeming the heretofore inadequate, misleading, and yet strangely persistent term "neo-orthodoxy."

1   Karl Barth
Christian Theology after Christendom

Karl Barth loved Mozart, but if one wished to compare this great composer of theology with a composer of music, it would have to be Beethoven. In 1822, after meeting Beethoven, a certain Herr Rochlitz wrote to his wife as follows:

> [H]e impressed me as being a man with a rich, aggressive intellect, an unlimited, never resting imagination. I saw him as one who, had he been cast on a desert isle when no more than a growing, capable boy, would have taken all he had lived and learned, all that had stuck to him in the way of knowledge, and there have meditated and brooded over his material until his fragments had become a whole, his imaginings turned to convictions which he would have shouted out into the world in all security and confidence.[1]

The whole (if I may!) "saga" of Karl Barth has fascinated me since I first began to read him fifty years ago, but two aspects of his work are particularly intriguing to me, as to many others: first, that he felt compelled to write so much—more, possibly, than any other single figure in the history of the faith—and second, that he did so as one who never abandoned his original intention to base everything on revelation, meaning supremely on the self-manifestation of God in Jesus Christ, as testified to in scripture. Some four years after Barth's death, I met one of his literary executors, his colleague the late Max Geiger, in France, and he told me: "We have discovered that Barth's *garage* is full of unpublished manuscripts. We have no idea how to deal with this!"

Barth himself understood this compulsion—biblically enough, one must say—as the consequence of a wonderful freedom. In one of his last writings he remarks,

Theology . . . demands free people . . . .

I have indeed become so free as to be able to write dogmatics—which many notable theologians are afraid of doing. Most theologians, especially today, write only little pamphlets and articles and Festschrift contributions. I was never content with this. I said to myself: "If I am a theologian I must try to work out broadly what I think I have perceived as God's revelation. What I think *I* have perceived. Yet not I as an individual but I as a member of the Christian church."

And then this characteristic note—the christological basis:

The last word I have to say . . . is not a concept like grace but a name: Jesus Christ. He is grace and he is the ultimate one beyond world and church and even theology. We cannot lay hold of him. But we have to do with him. And my own concern in my long life has been increasingly to emphasize this name and to say, "In him." There is no salvation but in this name. In him is grace. In him is the spur to work, warfare, and fellowship. In him is all that I have attempted in my life in weakness and folly. It is there in him.[2]

To many, both the breadth and immensity of Barth's work and the specificity (not to say narrowness) of the foundation upon which, avowedly, he builds this great spiritual edifice have been stumbling blocks. Is it not a matter of sheer presumption that anyone should claim to know so much about God? And is it not thoroughly speculative when such a one essays to base everything upon a Source, the entire written record of whom could quite easily be inserted into one of the small-print sections of just one of the fourteen volumes of *Church Dogmatics,* and hardly increase its thickness by a millimeter? And is it not a case of arrogance, besides, when this same person spurns all attempts at Christian apologetics, and heaps scorn upon what he calls (*mixophilosophicotheologia*," namely, "the mixture of philosophy and theology which, at present, seems to make such a tremendous impression upon many as the newest thing under the sun"?[3]

What is usually not understood by those who voice such criticism of Karl Barth is what I shall attempt to clarify in this essay:

namely that early in his professional career, and quite consistently throughout it, Barth was led to the realization that Christianity as it has been permitted to conduct itself throughout most of its historical sojourn—imperial Christianity; Christianity as the official cultus of the West; Christianity as the *corpus christianum*—had in reality, its vestiges notwithstanding, come to an effective end; and, in consequence, that from now on it would be necessary for the community gathered around the name of Jesus Christ to base its life, its mission, and its theological understanding quite literally "on grace alone, through faith alone," "*per Christum solum.*"

This explanation of Barth's alleged "positivism of revelation" (Bonhoeffer), "fideism," and "Christomonism," as well as his determination to explore the lengths and breadths of Christian doctrine with such unprecedented thoroughness, has impressed itself upon me with renewed force as I read again many of his own words— words that in some ways I, too, had forgotten. I would like to draw attention to four passages from Barth's work, taken from different periods in his life, that testify quite explicitly to his consciousness of finding himself at the edge of a new era, one in which it would not only be impossible but also, often enough, dangerous and even blasphemous for Christians to assume any real continuity, from the world's side, between their gospel and the still reputedly Christian civilization. In order to let Barth's own words speak for themselves, I shall confine myself to documentary evidence of this consciousness; the point could also be made, of course, biographically.

First, and proceeding chronologically, we should consider the influence of two earlier thinkers on the mind of the young Swiss pastor: Søren Kierkegaard and Franz Overbeck. The name of Kierkegaard is well known today, though few enough of those who know and use this name have any profound knowledge of the man's thought, which even today is capable of shocking bourgeois Christian sensibilities. Barth began to be "seriously" aware of Kierkegaard in 1919:

The first book by this man which I bought—it was then 1909—
was *The Moment*. I assume that I also read it then. But it cannot
have made a very profound impression on me. He only entered
my thinking seriously, and more extensively, in 1919, at the
critical turning-point between the first and second editions of
my *Romans*; after that he could be seen in a more important role
in my other literary works. . . . What we found particularly attractive, delightful and instructive was his inexorable criticism,
which went on snipping and snipping. We saw him using it to
attack all speculation which wiped out the infinite qualitative
difference between God and man. Thus in that second phase of
our revolution he was one of the cocks whose voice seemed to
proclaim to us from near and far the dawn of a really new day.[4]

Apart from "a few individuals," Barth remarked later, "Kierkegaard
. . . did not have the slightest influence on 19th-century theology."[5]
He was wholly out of place in an atmosphere where "[t]here was
scarcely a theologian who did not also consider himself a professional philosopher."[6]

Nineteenth-century theology worked on the general assumption
that relatedness to the world is its primary task and on the specific assumption that there is a possibility for general acceptance
of the Christian faith.[7]

The world that had manifested itself to Barth and his friend Eduard
Thurneysen and a few other Christian pastors and thinkers by 1919
was by no means one that gave evidence of such a "general acceptance"; therefore, as is well known, in the second edition of his
literary bombshell, the *Römerbrief*, it was to Kierkegaard that
Barth turned in his attempt to explain himself to his critics:

[I]f I have a system, it is limited to a recognition of what
Kierkegaard called the "infinite qualitative distinction" between
time and eternity, and to my regarding this as possessing negative as well as positive significance: "God is in heaven, and thou
art on earth."[8]

The influence of Franz Overbeck on Barth's developing consciousness of the distinction between Christianity and culture

(*Christianity and Culture*, not incidentally, was the title assigned to the posthumously published remains of Overbeck's literary work) is less well known, yet in some ways still more interesting. There is a fascinating reference to Overbeck in the same Preface to the second edition of the commentary on *Romans* from which I have just quoted. In fact, in that place Barth acknowledges that "the man Overbeck" is second only to Paul himself (!) in having brought about the significant changes between the first and second editions of this epoch-making study:

> Elsewhere, Eduard Thurneysen and I have drawn attention, at some length, to the warning address by Overbeck to all theologians. This warning I have first applied to myself, and then directed upon the enemy. Whether I have dealt at all adequately with the questions raised by this eminent and pious man I must leave to the judgment of those who are able to perceive the nature of the riddle he has formulated so precisely, and are willing at least to attempt its solution.[9]

Franz Overbeck, who died in 1905, was professor of critical theology in the University of Basel, and a close friend of Friedrich Nietzsche. It is significant that Barth, in the statement I have just cited, refers to Overbeck as "this eminent and pious man," because he was by no means so regarded generally; indeed, recently I found him described straightforwardly as "an atheist" in one encyclopedia. One "had only to mention [his name] in Basel at that time to make everyone's hair stand on end," Barth observed later, and he spoke of Overbeck as this "strange alien."[10]

If Kierkegaard's declaration that the official Christianity of Europe was "a forgery" seems strong even today, Overbeck's analysis was still more drastic. According to him (*as quoted by Barth*), "all Christian theology, from the Patristic Age onward, is unchristian and satanic, for its draws Christianity into the sphere of civilization and culture, and thereby denies the essentially eschatological character of the Christian religion."[11] Barth was too nuanced a thinker even in his youth to accept such a grand historical generalization; yet, as Thurneysen writes, "Barth felt a kinship with Overbeck's insights," and, "despite much head-shaking and opposition" in response to the study of Overbeck that Barth published in 1920,[12] Thurneysen insists that Barth "understood [Overbeck] basically aright when he saw through his outward profession of scepticism to his real intentions"—which were, for Barth, the honorable intentions of preserving authentic faith from the distortions of imperial religion.[13]

Incidentally—or perhaps not so incidentally, after all—apropos the term "neo-orthodoxy," in February of 1924 Barth wrote to his friend Thurneysen as follows:

> [T]o me the shadow of orthodoxy in which we necessarily stand for the moment presents the most painful problem of the situation. I was overjoyed in Bern at the citation of Overbeck which I had introduced at one point and which saved me from an all too unconditional approval by Hadorn. Also Hofmann had to concede that "our" position is not simply a return to "conscience-enslaving" orthodoxy. In this connection the liberal resistance concerns me far less than the fact that one necessarily finds himself in a certain remoteness in relation to the humanists and the socialists.[14]

In both Kierkegaard and Overbeck, Barth found support for his growing suspicion, which was confirmed for him by events associated with the Great War, that Christendom was in a state of disintegration, and that Christianity could only survive by distinguishing itself markedly from the *corpus christianum*.

The second documentary evidence of Barth's growing awareness of the demise of Christendom and of the implications of this event for Christian theology and practice is the little booklet on baptism. It is a statement that has embarrassed all the Protestant churches, even, I think, Baptists. But it warrants very serious consideration by all who share Barth's reading of the *Zeitgeist* and who must therefore ask themselves whether the practice of infant baptism as normative can be justified today.

The booklet is a translation from the German *Die kirchliche Lehre von der Taufe,* which in turn is the transcription of a lecture that Barth gave at Gwatt am Thunersee in May of 1943.[15] Unlike the Anabaptists, Barth is unwilling to say that "baptism without the willingness and readiness of the baptized" is "ineffectual"; but, he states, while it may be "true" it is "not correct," for "it is not done in obedience, it is not administered according to proper order, and therefore it is necessarily clouded baptism."[16] He admits that *baptismus infantium* was already "acknowledged" in the second century, that it became "general" after the establishment, and that it was "defended with great energy by the Reformers."[17] He considers the alleged arguments from scripture, none of which he finds convincing as genuine exegesis,[18] and also the extra-scriptural reasons why the baptism of children is held to be desirable — among them, the concept of its being a concrete illustration of the Reformation teaching *sola gratia* (an argument, Barth says, that none of the Reformers themselves used).[19]

Then he comes to the heart of the matter:

> Am I wrong in thinking that the really operative extraneous ground for infant-baptism, even with the Reformers, and ever and again quite plainly since, has been this: one did not want then in any case or at any price to deny the existence of the evangelical Church in the Constantinian *corpus christianum* — and today one does not want to renounce the present form of the national church [*Volkskirche*]? . . . Has not the anxiety, which here shows itself, often unconsciously, the quite primitive form to which Luther openly confessed on occasion: there would not be too many people baptized if, instead of being *brought* to baptism, they had to come of their own accord?[20]

Conscious of the fact that all three of the greatest villains of the age, Hitler, Mussolini, and Stalin, were baptized at infancy, the critical theologian, expelled from Nazi Germany and by now teaching in his hometown of Basel, asks:

> Are we so sure of the inner worth of the Constantinian system and of the present day form of the National Church — is our conscience in these matters so clear — that we ought and must resolve to hold fast to them, at whatever cost — even at the cost of

inflicting wounds and weakness on the Church through a disorderly baptism? Or, on the contrary, does not the unmistakable disorder of our baptismal practice show at once just this: that there is a disorder in the sociological structure of our Church, which perhaps must still be endured for a long time, but which can in no case be cited as a serious argument against the better ordering of our baptismal practice? *Where does it stand written that Christians may not be in the minority, perhaps a very small minority? Might they not be of more use to their surroundings, if they were allowed to be a healthy Church? What is really wanted for the Church to remain a National Church in the present-day sense of the term:* a Church *of* the people, instead of a Church *for* the people? Theology has to state that the pressing issue of a better ordering of our baptismal practice is relevant to the question how that may come about. . . . What is wanted is very simple: instead of the present infant-baptism, a baptism which on the part of the baptized is *a responsible act.*[21]

I cite this pamphlet more because of what it tells us about Barth's assessment of Christendom than because of his baptismal theology. Yet the two concerns are obviously closely related, and it has always seemed to me unfortunate that Protestants in the past have been so offended by Barth's critique of baptismal practices that they were oblivious to the historical and ecclesiological reflection behind it. Perhaps half a century later more of us have had enough experience of God's providential questioning of Christendom to become a little more imaginative also in our theology of baptism.

The third segment of Barth's writing to which I would like to refer is found in his magnum opus, the *Church Dogmatics,* volume I, part 2.[22] This part-volume, which did not appear in English translation until 1956, the work of translation having been interrupted by the war, was published in German in the fateful year 1939. The segment from which I shall quote has to do with one of Barth's favorite subjects, religion.

In contrast to Paul Tillich, religion was for Barth a mainly neg-

ative concept and reality. It is the attempt of frightened, unbeliev-
ing, security- and power-seeking humankind to take heaven by
storm, to control the Controller, to attain permanence and *securitas*. It is Babel in strict contradistinction to Pentecost. As such, it
should never be interpreted as the correlate of revelation. To the
contrary,

> Because it is a grasping, religion is the contradiction of revela-
> tion, the concentrated expression of human unbelief, i.e., an at-
> titude and activity which is directly opposed to faith. It is a feeble
> but defiant, an arrogant but hopeless, attempt to create something
> which man could do, but now cannot do, or can do only because
> and if God himself creates it for him: the knowledge of the truth,
> the knowledge of God. We cannot, therefore, interpret the at-
> tempt as a harmonious co-operating of man with the revelation
> of God, as though religion were a kind of outstretched hand
> which is filled by God in His revelation.[23]

The religious quest is a quest for power, but the only power that
belongs to the revelation of which Jesus Christ is the center is "a
power [that] dwells in weakness."[24]

This contrast between power-seeking religion and "apostolic
weakness" now becomes the point of departure for one of those
lengthy and often insightful small-print excursuses (some of which
are attributed by some to Barth's longtime friend and assistant,
Charlotte von Kirschbaum).[25] In this one, the author intends to
show that the history of the *Christian* religion, which is no less a
religion (ergo a product of unbelief!) than any other, is in reality
an admixture of two incompatible elements: a dominant strain of
power-grasping religion and a never-*quite*-discarded recall of the
very different response, faith, that is elicited by divine revelation.

The author divides the history of Christianity into three periods:
During the first, up to the time of Constantine, the Christian movement "had one great advantage": namely, as an illicit and oppressed
faith, it was not able externally to embrace the full *modus operandi*
of religion, but was "as it were, automatically forced into something
like the apostolic position, i.e., the apostolic weakness."[26] This does

not mean that we can consider this period a golden age, however, to which, romantically, we should try to return; for while the early Christians were excluded from power, they give many indications of desiring it with all their hearts. For instance, in the "early self-commendations of Christianity" produced by the apologists of the second and third centuries, "a remarkably small part is played by the fact that *grace* is the truth of Christianity, that the Christian is justified when he is without God, like Abraham, that he is like the publican in the temple, the prodigal son, wretched Lazarus, the guilty thief crucified with Jesus Christ."[27] "Still, the early church was compelled constantly to reflect and to return to that which is ultimate and real."[28]

But that saving necessity "came to an end with the developments which took place after Constantine and it quite disappeared in the whole period which was dominated by the idea of the *Corpus Christianum*."[29] The second, centuries-long period provided the church with the opportunity to explore to the hilt the possibilities of *religion*—to be, in relation to the state, a second "world-power," and wherever possible "to try to become the first and real world-power instead of the second." And here Barth raises historical questions that ought still to be pondered very earnestly today, and the more so in view of our increasingly pluralistic context:

> Where was the awareness of grace as the truth of Christianity in the days of the investiture-conflict and the crusades, or in the world of Gothic? To what extent was this a real concern in the great reform movement of Cluny and monasticism generally? To what extent could heathen and Jews find in the medieval Church a power that was genuinely different, a novel and unfamiliar power, not the power which men can always demonstrate, but the power of God which humbles and therefore blesses all men, the power of the Gospel? To what extent could the Church confront the Islam which oppressed it in South and East as something which was really original?[30]

It is true, says the author, that even during the long centuries from Constantine to the Renaissance, "The evidence of grace was not destroyed. It maintained its quiet force. Even in this world revelation shone out in the spiritual poverty of those who believed it as it is meant to be believed. But it did so in the Church only against the Church (i.e., against the tendency which dominated the Church, against the proud but treacherous idea of the *corpus christianum*)."[31]

The third period is the modern. It is marked by the gradual but inevitable breakdown of Christendom: "Western humanity has come of age, or thinks it has. . . . The floods have receded, and behold, there is nothing much left after the thousand years of the apparent domination of Christianity except a little monotheism, morality, and mysticism."[32]

Following the termination of "the medieval dream," "even Protestantism had . . . to adapt itself to the existence of a religious society [i.e., the organized church] which modern man regards as ultimately unnecessary and innocuous." Having for so long found its destiny as the official cultus of Western peoples, the Christian religion now "took up the role alloted to it, and was at pains to make itself indispensable." It did so, says Barth (with an irony worthy of Kierkegaard),

> by pointing out and demonstrating that if there is a truth in the Christian religion which can profitably be heard and believed, especially in the modern age, it consists in this, that properly understood, the doctrine of Jesus Christ, and the way of life which corresponds to it, has the secret power of giving to man the inward capacity to seek and attain the aims and purposes which he has independently chosen.[33]

Pursuing this approach, the Christian church in the third period achieved "many victories—more than would have been dreamed at the peak of the period in the 18th Century. . . . But no one should be deceived about the fact that they were Pyrrhic victories. And the no less numerous reverses, which [the church] suffered on the same road, were more significant of the real state of things than the victories."[34]

Barth concludes this remarkable mini–church history, the "history of this contradiction," with a challenge that he was evidently attempting to inspire in his readers and in the remnants of Christendom: Will a *fourth* period demonstrate a potentiality in the Christian community for anything that could contradict this contradiction? And he answers: Only if Christianity were "to set its hope wholly and utterly on grace" could this occur:

> Notwithstanding the contradiction and therefore our own existence, we can and must perceive that for our part we and our contradiction against grace stand under the even more powerful contradiction of grace itself. We can and must—in faith.[35]

My fourth and final instance of Barth's commanding sense of the changed situation of Christianity in the world, and the challenges that this implied for him, is taken from a letter that he addressed to an unnamed pastor in a part of the world, the German Democratic Republic, where Christians could no longer pretend that the situation remained unchanged and that Christendom was still intact.

In concluding this letter, which was first published in Germany in 1958, and which achieved among many of my friends in the former East Germany almost the status of a biblical exhortation, Barth remarked:

> What a multitude of things we have taken for granted: a church occupying a comfortable place in the social structure, her existence guaranteed, or at least respected, or at the very least tolerated by society in general and by the state in particular! Sunday as a recognized holiday and day of rest, and the chief church festivals which have somehow left their impact on the life of the people as a whole; infant baptism, confirmation, marriage, and burial, the Christian landmarks of the milieu and the existence of Mr. Everyman—means whereby the church has liked to reassure herself again and again of her obvious indispensability! The influence of the church in public education, instruction and upbringing of young people . . . The prestige or at least the dignity of her official representatives among the leaders of other social and cultural organizations. The formal recognition of the

church's freedom to participate in the discussion of general human concerns as a direct or indirect partner, welcome or unwelcome. Although these privileges of Christianity have never and nowhere gone unchallenged, certainly not in the last few centuries, it has seemed to us the most natural thing in the world that the proclamation of the gospel of Jesus Christ should continue to run in some such channels as these, and that we should do the utmost for their preservation and defence, for the sake of God and the gospel! . . . Is the world as such obligated to grant to Christianity the right to maintain that form of existence in its midst?[36]

Referring in conclusion to a statement of the East German superintendent of the district of Cottbus, who had recently assured his fellow Christians that they were living "at the end of the Constantinian era," Barth averred that, having "a certain wariness about all theoretical formulations of a philosophy of history," he would "hesitate to make this expression [his] own"—a caveat that strikes one as somewhat precious in view of the kind of historical schema to which we have just listened from the *Dogmatics*! Nevertheless, he continued, "something resembling this approaching end begins to show itself dimly everywhere, but very sharply in your part of the world."[37] But this should by no means be received in the spirit of defeat and sorrow, for "the continuance and victory of the cause of God . . . is not unconditionally linked with the forms of existence which [the Christian church] has had until now."

[T]he hour may strike and has perhaps already struck when God, to our discomfiture, but to his glory and for the salvation of mankind, will put an end to this mode of existence because it lacks integrity and has lost its usefulness. Yes, it could be our duty to free ourselves inwardly from our dependency on that mode of existence even while it still lasts. Indeed, on the assumption that it may one day entirely disappear, we definitely should look about us for new ventures and new directions.[38]

In keeping with my intention to consider these "remembered voices" from the perspective of our own search for guidance and hope, I will conclude by translating this challenge into terms that relate to our context—a context that is externally quite different from that of the pastor to whom Karl Barth wrote, but at a more subtle level of perception one containing many similarities. Like that pastor, many of us in parishes, church offices, seminaries, and elsewhere are frequently dismayed by the metamorphosis that is now, also in North America, overtaking old Christendom. We have been considering in these pages a theologian (according to Pope Pius XII the greatest theologian since Thomas Aquinas!) who evidently struggled with this great ecclesiastical "paradigm shift" already early in his professional career. I have argued that his whole theological outpouring must be seen as a response to that transition. That in itself ought to constitute a source of encourage-ment to all who are tempted to think that, after the glories of Chris-tendom, Christianity may have little appeal to the human spirit and intellect.

A recent *Christian Century* article suggests that Barth is per-haps *the* "postmodern" theologian, anticipating as he did so much of "postmodernity's critique of Enlightened reason."[39] It is more to the point, I should say, to see him as a post-*Christendom* theo-logian, who critiqued not only Enlightenment rationality but the whole phenomenon of a Christian establishment that had always seduced believers into seeking the approval of *whatever* the dom-inant society regarded as reasonable.

Barth found it possible to enter the post-Constantinian world or-der without illusion, but with hope, because, in being denied the "religious" condolences of his liberal teachers, he was driven back to the biblical, preestablishment, transcultural foundations of the faith. Thus *theology,* intentionally separated from the usual philo-sophic and political props, became for him, not merely a profes-sional task but a matter of life and death—the thread upon which the church's future hung—a conception of the Christian life beau-tifully symbolized in the title of the journal that he helped to found, *Theologische Existenz heute* (Theological existence today).

Recently, an American seminary president said to me: "We are terrified and debilitated by the reductions to which the churches are now being subjected." And one wonders, remembering Karl Barth: has our fear of the future anything to do with the fact that theology is still for us, largely, the occupation of a few—something that, so far as the daily life of the churches is concerned, can be reduced to slogans that echo the continually changing interests, concerns, trends, and values of the culture at large? May it not be that the only real hope for this province of the Christian Oecumene, which adapted itself all too uncritically to a Modernity that it still feebly champions, is finally to overcome what Karl Barth was wont to call "the children's disease of being ashamed of theology?" At the end of "the Christian century" are we perhaps ready, in a way that we were not ready halfway through it, to lay claim to the legacy of Barth? Not, one hopes, to reiterate his words, but to be instructed and edified by them? In our incipiently "terrified and debilitated" state, however repressed it may be, can we discover in our midst also the will to explore more expectantly the possibilities inherent in the faith we confess, and thus to disengage ourselves sufficiently from our host society to become of some real use to it in its own struggle to find a way into the future?

Paul Tillich
Systematic Theology—
Faith's Quest for Wholeness

It was, I believe, one of the most providential accidents of my theological education that when I was Paul Tillich's student in the 1950s I was deeply under the spell of Karl Barth. Consequently, as I sat in Tillich's lectures and seminars, I argued with him silently all the while, and, as a result, I learned a great deal from him. I highly recommend this method of pedagogy.

Lest this autobiographical reference reinforce a common misconception, however, let me at once enter a caveat. It has been usual to contrast these two "remembered voices" of the earlier part of this century as though they were almost diametrically opposed to each other. But from the perspective of nearly half a century one must recognize this for the exaggeration that it is. Tillich himself, after he visited Karl Barth in Basel on December 1, 1963, less than two years before Tillich's death, reported to his friend and biographer Wilhelm Pauck, "Barth and I are friends again!" Pauck asked what evidence there was for this, and Tillich replied, "He accompanied me to the tram halt."[1] Markus Barth told me later that after this historic last visit Tillich had felt that "Your father and I now say the same thing. He is undoubtedly more kerygmatic than I, but it comes to the same thing."

This testimony may represent the sense of harmony that is sometimes granted to old age, or, as John Coleman Bennett once suggested, it may be another instance of Tillich's propensity to incorporate other people and views into his own very expansive schema. I do think, however, that the differences between the two contemporaries have been overdone, and that with the benefit of hindsight one may detect strong lines of convergence between these Protestant giants of our immediate past—among such, their common recall and lively deployment of the Protestant Reformers.[2] One may readily grant that while Barth listened with special care to Calvin, Tillich was a spiritual child of Martin Luther. And one may note the differences that stem from that dual lineage, including their varying attitudes toward the Bible, the capacity or incapacity of the finite for the infinite (the latter being the famous *extra calvinisticum*), the relation of reason and revelation, and many other matters. Yet in their political[3] as in their theological histories, Barth and Tillich are at least close enough that their conversation on December 1, 1963, would not have had to restrict itself to the pleasantries of shared memories and the civilities of good breeding.

Paul Tillich was a decidedly *systematic* theologian. There is some truth in the frequently expressed opinion that systematic theology is a presumptuous and dangerous undertaking. But is it not also a necessary one? Both Barth and Tillich were impelled by their awareness of the great transformation through which the Christian movement was passing to try once more, in the face of this change, to articulate the faith in something like its fullness. Their ways of doing this differ, and in some aspects markedly so, but that they did it at all must give *us* pause. For half a century later we find ourselves in a period that not only has difficulty seeing things whole but tends, in some of its most allegedly advanced expressions, thoroughly to distrust any articulation of wholeness.

Consider, for example, the following characterization of the postmodernism alluded to in the previous chapter: postmodernism "engenders the suspicion that the desire for consensus so characteristic of the scientific worldview is a phallocratic and universalizing one . . . , a desire to suppress heterogeneity."[4]

To be sure, the suspicion that any carefully wrought interpretation of reality may lead to the suppression of "otherness" is by no means without foundation. Not only has the present century witnessed the advent of political systems whose ironclad consistency has entailed "solutions" that, in their enactment, meant quite literally the elimination of millions of human beings who did not fit the alleged necessities of historical destiny, but, beyond that, the most perceptive among us have had the insight to recognize what Reinhold Niebuhr called the "ideological taint" in all human thinking. Dorothee Sölle defines ideology as "a system of propositional truths independent of the situation, a superstructure no longer relevant to praxis, to the situation, to the real questions of life."[5]

Theology is by no means immune from the temptation to ideology, and the more cohesive and omnibus it tries to be, the more conspicuously it courts this temptation. Yet the alternative to the *search* for wholeness seems equally untenable, and in the end may prove more damaging. For theological reflection that remains content with random observations, aphorisms, stories, or fragments of the whole not only begs the question of its own ground and inner consistency but threatens always to divide and destroy the community of faith. The medieval scholastic feeling for the unity of truth that gave rise to systematic theology is not incidental to Christianity, no matter how falsely it may be *used* by those driven by the quest for power. If at the core of this faith there is a confession of the triune oneness of the deity, the "integrity of the creation," the unity of the "body of Christ," the reconciliation and ultimate re-uniting of all alienated beings, and similar emphases, then to refrain from striving for an adequate expression of this unity and harmony is at least irresponsible, even if boasting that one has actually grasped it in its fullness comes close to blasphemy.

Sameness has its dangers, but so does difference. In its watchfulness against imposed uniformity, the skeptical mood of our age has encouraged a cult of diversity that often seems oblivious to the problems of plurality. In the name of celebrating sheer difference and otherness, some would like to see the church embrace whatever is "meaningful" to people. It is remarked that our situation in the post-Christendom world is very like that of the early Christians prior to the "establishment" of the fourth century. It is noted that in the early church there were many possibilities and variations

where both practice and theory were concerned, and that confor-
mity of doctrine, polity, and practice must be associated in particular with the transformation of the church into the official cultus
of the imperium. And there is truth in this: we dare not forget, for
example, that the Council of Nicaea was called and convened by
an emperor who feared the breakup of the imperium and saw in the
Christian faith, with its monotheism and its preference for the res-
olution of all dichotomies, a highly desirable cultus.

But that kind of historical justification for honoring difference
within and around the Christian religion today conveniently ne-
glects to notice that already prior to the establishment there were,
fortunately, persons of insight like Irenaeus (not to mention Paul!)
who realized that without some sustained attempt to delineate the
core meaning of the faith the Christian movement would quickly
disappear in a shower of mutually exclusive interpretations and
quarreling factions. It very nearly did! Formal theology may always court blasphemy. But we can be quite certain that, had it not
been for the Pauls and Augustines and Anselms and Thomases and
Calvins and Schleiermachers and Barths of this tradition there
would be no tradition in any sense of the term *singular* enough to
have prevented ultimate fragmentation and dissipation at almost
any given point in the evolution of Christianity. The fifteen hundred (or is it four or five thousand?) different denominations and
sects on the North American continent alone bear eloquent testimony to the strong predisposition of religion (and remember
Barth's critique of religion) to proliferate endlessly, and thus—at
least in the case of *this* religion—to destroy the very mutuality,
communality, reconciliation, and forbearing love that is both its
means and its end.

Theology in North America today seems rather to reflect than
to correct the potentially chaotic tendencies of both cultural and religious diversity. While there are those among us who endeavor to
keep alive the art of what is called by the unsatisfactory name of
"systematic theology," the trend-setting theologies in our media-
driven society are clearly those that take up specific causes, iden-

tities, and themes, and, to make way for these, engage in elaborate labors of deconstructing what has been handed over from the past, especially the more comprehensive systems of doctrine.

Among the objects of this exercise in disassembling dogma and identifying its hidden functions, the theological heritage of the "neo-orthodox" is often targeted. One recognizes, of course, that every generation has to engage in a struggle with the previous generation in order both to free itself from the excessive authority of its teachers, now immortalized, and to address realities that its teachers could not possibly have anticipated. But it seems to me that the effect of the present disengagement has exceeded necessity. The impression has too often been created, not only that these forebears, being children of time, were sometimes myopic and lacking in both self-knowledge and wisdom, but that their whole enterprise, namely the work of theological reconstruction as such, was questionable. Thus the intellectual curiosity, passion for connectedness, and quest for wholeness of understanding that these same teachers of the faith inspired in my generation of theological students has been exchanged in today's seminary classrooms for an atmosphere of vigilance in the face of every potential violation of some particularity by some attempt at universality. As Douglas Sloan has written in his book *Faith and Knowledge,* "The collapse of the theological renaissance [i.e., the 'neo-orthodox' movement we are recalling here] left in its wake a diversity of fractured theologies. A less generous observer has dubbed them 'special interest theologies.'" Sloan links this with the aforementioned postmodernity, which, whatever it may mean beyond the fact that it is after modernity, seems to entail a capitulation to "relativism and subjectivism" born of the insight that "there is no truth."[6]

Because at the core of the Christian confession there is the claim that Truth, with capital T, *lives* ("I am the Truth") and therefore may not be reduced to propositions, theories, and systems, the postmodern denial of truth as human possibility is nearer to the kingdom of heaven than were modern pretentions to truth's mastery and finality. But neither alternative, surely, can be embraced by

Christians. "Faith," as Barth heard Anselm of Canterbury saying, "seeks understanding," and understanding has fundamentally to do with the grasping of—or as Tillich would have said, "being grasped *by*"—the interrelatedness of all that is. What medieval thinkers called the "beatific vision"—seeing the ultimate no longer "through a glass darkly" but "face to face," which is to say complete understanding—is indeed an eschatological one; but faith, though not sight, *drives toward* [*quaerens*] just that fullness of comprehension, and the life of discipleship within the *koinonia* requires at least a sufficient insight and commonly held vision of the whole to enable mutuality of decision and action in relation to its parts.

The question with which these reflections leave us could be stated thus: How, in an age that is increasingly skeptical of all unified systems, since they so regularly turn into ideologies that mask quests for power, is one to maintain the theological pursuit of the unity of truth? Specifically, are there ways of ensuring that systematic expressions of Christian teaching may discourage co-optation by power and sustain openness, both to the mystery that refuses to give itself fully to any attempt at comprehension and to other ways of perceiving that mystery?

My argument here will be that Paul Tillich proffered a response to this concern that is permanently viable and especially worthy of our contemplation today. Tillich insists that Christian theology is inherently propelled toward comprehensiveness, yet there are important vehicles of self-correction in Tillich's quest for wholeness which prevent the system from becoming closed and oppressive. I shall elaborate on that claim by employing, as much as possible, Tillich's own words or those of his commentators.

Paul Tillich's impulse to comprehensiveness emerged early in his career. Wilhelm Pauck, in his book *From Luther to Tillich: The Reformers and Their Heirs,* a work that contains the extended fragment that was to have been the second volume of his Tillich biography, relates the manner in which, while a theological student at

the University of Halle, Tillich approached the task of construct-
ing a statement of purpose for the religious fraternity Wingolf, one
of the three most significant early influences on his development.
The motto of the Wingolfbund was *Di henos panta,* "all through
One"—the "One" being Christ. At Halle, however, "the fellowship . . . was troubled by the question of what the Christian principle [expressed in this motto] meant spiritually and practically for
the common life." Tillich, who became the presiding officer of this
unit of the fraternity, set about to articulate an answer to this:

> His skill in formulating definitions and distinctions and his pas-
> sion for clear and coherent thinking were now put to the test.
> The results of his efforts never ceased to be vividly remembered
> by him. "The question of the principles of a Christian commu-
> nity," he wrote later, "was so thoroughly argued out in the group
> that all who were active in the struggle profited a great deal by
> it. At that time, I came to understand the value of objective state-
> ments like denominational creeds. When a community gives
> general recognition to a confessional basis whose meaning tran-
> scends subjective belief or doubt, it will hold together even
> while allowing room for tendencies toward doubt, criticism, and
> uncertainty."[7]

Writing to his father about this attempt to formulate a position,
the young Tillich declared: "I am about to construct the first 'dogmatics' of my life. . . . It is to be a brief but substantial exposition
of the Wingolfite ideal."[8] It is interesting to note what the budding
dogmatician recommended: First, that "the basis of Christian community must be the message of the Bible, objectively understood
and kept independent from subjective arbitrariness."

> He rejected a selective as well as a literal interpretation of the
> Bible and suggested that the content of the Bible should be com-
> prehensively expressed in a few brief biblical terms, in effect,
> in the form of a creed saying that the biblical witness presents
> to men Jesus Christ as their only Lord and Redeemer.

> Second, he expressed the belief "that personal doubt or indecision
> should be tolerated." Those who found themselves unable to accept

the creed for themselves should not be excluded. So long as they were willing to participate in a community for which such a creed represented its basis and purpose, they could be fully part of it.

Third, with respect to the latter, their doubt must be tolerated, not only on humanitarian grounds but because "faith embraces itself as well as doubt about itself." By doubt, the young theologian did not mean merely intellectual misgivings but what he later would call "existential doubt." The only condition that would have to be met by the doubters, he believed, is that they should remain "seriously concerned about [their] doubt."[9]

We encounter already here some of the main themes that must inform our exposition of Tillich's response to our question about theological systems. He seems never to have entertained the idea that a serious Christian thinker could be satisfied with anything less than the attempt at clear, interconnected, coherent—that is to say, systematic—theology, nor that the church, which the Wingolf experience (he said) enabled him to understand,[10] could survive without such thinking. It was therefore painful to him that the actual writing of a systematic theology—a task that he set for himself very early in his life—had for so long to be put off, and was so drastically interrupted by events beyond his control. So in the preface to the first volume of *Systematic Theology,* which he finally managed to publish in 1951, the first sentences read:

> For a quarter of a century I have wanted to write a systematic theology. It always has been impossible for me to think theologically in any other than a systematic way. The smallest problem, if taken seriously and radically, drove me to all other problems and to the anticipation of a whole in which they could find solution. But world history, personal destiny, and special problems kept me from fulfilling this self-chosen task.[11]

This drive to comprehensiveness and systematic expression may be in part a token of Tillich's German-ness, but it also has deeper historical roots. In the work already cited, Pauck titles his chapter on Tillich "Paul Tillich: Heir of the Nineteenth Century." Like many of his contemporaries, Tillich felt a special bond with the romantic movement of the nineteenth century. He often told his North American classes, "In America, you never had a nineteenth century." This greatly baffled and half-offended most of us. Certainly we had had a nineteenth century! Some of us felt, indeed, that our highly industrialized society, as well as our liberal Protestant churches, had had far too much of the nineteenth century—witness our sentimental hymns and religious art! What we did not realize was that for the European Tillich "the nineteenth century" connoted neither industrialism nor sentimentality, primarily, but a sustained and courageous attempt to "see life whole" on the part of philosophers, artists, and theologians who were rebelling against the truncation of reason and the fragmentation of existence under the auspices of the Enlightenment and its technological offspring. Indeed, Tillich's quarrel with America (which he nevertheless came to appreciate) was in some ways a quarrel with the Enlightenment, the practical effects of which were so significant for the formation of the United States in particular. With its simultaneous elevation and reduction of reason, its loss of categories and symbols for explaining the continuing darkness of existence, and its too easy distinctions between good and evil, the Enlightenment in its New World expression robbed people of their human need to contemplate the mystery of the whole.

Like the leaders of "the romantic rebellion" (Sir Kenneth Clark) themselves, Tillich looked back behind "enlightened" modernity to the medieval world. He loved the Middle Ages because of their approximation of what he called "theonomy"—that is, the harmonization of the independent (autonomous) and extraneous (heteronomous) dimensions of creaturely existence.

> Theonomous periods are periods in which rational autonomy is preserved in law and knowledge, in community and art. Where there is theonomy nothing which is considered true and just is sacrificed. Theonomous periods do not feel split, but *whole and centered*. Their center is neither their autonomous freedom nor their heteronomous authority but the depth of reason ecstatically experienced and symbolically expressed.[12]

Though he may indeed have been "heir of the nineteenth century," and though he may be said to have lived "on the boundary"[13] between the nineteenth and twentieth centuries, Tillich was thoroughly and even painfully rooted in the present. His celebrated sympathy for existentialism as well as the perilous course of his own life made him well aware that ours is *not* a theonomous period but, on the contrary, one in which there is precisely a feeling of being "split"—what one commentator recently dubbed our "cineplexed" character. It was this awareness that caused Tillich to develop hamartiology along the lines that he did: sin as "estrangement" and "alienation." But he believed it to be the aim of the Christian message to confront and, so far as possible, *overcome* such disjointedness and fragmentation through the recovery of the theonomous condition. Therefore it was in his view all the more mandatory for Christian theology in such a period to articulate that message in an integrated, reasonable, and engaged manner, always attempting to correlate the human question with the revelatory answer. In short, far from being "a system of propositional truths independent of the situation" (Sölle), the system Tillich worked out was—at least in his own mind—a *response* to "the situation," namely, the situation of a broken and bewildered civilization in danger of disintegration.

Tillich's own sense of being an "answering theologian," responding to the human predicament even through the systematic *form* of his work, did not, of course, prevent others from seeing it as the superimposition of an a priori religious position upon the raw stuff of existence. His critics said to him, in effect, "You pretend to make a correlation between the human question and the divine answer, but obviously your formulation of the question is already determined by the answer that you intend to give from the side of religious faith." Or, conversely, if they were religiously conservative, they said: "You tailor your theological *answers* to the humanistic questions you have predetermined on the basis of what is, after all, your own limited experience of historical existence. In this way you dilute the gospel and overlook its radical discontinuity with *all* alleged preparation for hearing it [*praeparatio evangelica*]."[14]

Tillich himself admitted that there were certain problems inherent in systems of theological thought *as systems*. In his reply to his critics in the 1952 Kegley and Bretall volume celebrating his work as "a kind of Protestant *Summa* for our time,"[15] Tillich addressed those who complained about the "formal character" of his thought:

> I can only answer with the words I often voice to my students: "Those of you who are most opposed to the system show least patience if they discover inconsistencies in my thought. The way to organize a group of ideas consistently is to put them into systematic form." But there is a real danger felt by those who are uneasy about the system; namely, that its form becomes self-sufficient and determines the content. Should this occur, the truth is molded till it fits the system. This is almost unavoidable in a deductive system, and there are deductive elements in every system. *As a corrective against this danger* I have begun each of the five parts with an existential analysis of the questions to which the theological concepts are supposed to furnish the answer. I do not doubt that in spite of this method there are passages in my systematic writings in which it is difficult to find the existential roots.[16]

In this statement we hear again what we began to hear from the young Wingolf theologian, namely, the insistence that systematic thinking applies to Christian theology as to any other attempt at understanding and communication: "The way to organize a group of ideas consistently is to put them into systematic form." But we also hear something new: a mature recognition that "the systematic form [may well] threaten to choke the living quality of . . . thought"—what Whitehead called "the livingness of reality." And we are told how the author of the system himself tries to correct this inherent difficulty: namely, instead of beginning each of the five parts of his systematic theology with a discussion of the doctrine it intends to elucidate, he begins by exploring that aspect of the human situation to which that particular dimension of Christian teaching wants to address itself.

For many years I was not convinced that such a procedure could serve as a deterrent to the aforementioned "ideological taint"— namely, the temptation to conduct the entire exercise, the so-called method of correlation, without constant reexposure to worldly actuality. Two particular emphases in Tillich's thought, however, eventually caused me to doubt my doubts about this.

The first is well-expressed in the introductory paragraph of chapter 2 of *Biblical Religion and the Search for Ultimate Reality*,[17] a little book in which Tillich attempted (some would say unsatisfactorily) to show that his approach to theology through a meditation on "being" (ontology), a heritage from the tradition of Athens, is entirely consistent with the more dramatic, historical or narrative approach of the tradition of Jerusalem. He writes:

> One can rightly say that man is the being who is able to ask questions. Let us think for a moment what it means to ask a question. It implies . . . that we do not have that for which we ask. If we had it, we would not ask for it. But, in order to be able to ask for something, we must have it partially; otherwise it could not be the object of a question. He who asks has and has not at the same time. If man is that being who asks the question of being, he has and does not have the being for which he asks.[18]

If this statement, which is typical of many others in the writings of Tillich, is considered carefully, it offsets the tendency of many of his readers to interpret the method of correlation as a superficial question-and-answer approach: human reason asks the question and divine revelation gives the answer. If it were that simple, then, as generations of catechumens would be ready to testify, it would be easy to compose the entire dialogue in advance, questions and answers alike, without reference to naked reality. But Tillich is not speaking here about specific questions, such as the Westminster Catechism's famous "What is the chief end of man?" He is using the language of question and answer metaphorically. What is important is not so much the questions that human beings *ask* as the question that the human being *is*. It is the *being* of the human that constitutes the question to which the answer is no dogma but only, correspondingly, the *being* of the One to whom dogma can only hesitatingly point: namely, the Christ as the bringer of "New Being." Moreover, as Tillich explains in his first volume of *Systematic Theology,* there is discontinuity as well as continuity between question and answer thus understood: the answer cannot be derived from the question (God remains transcendent), nor can the question be derived from the answer, that is, from some previous articulation of it.

This has importance for our concern that there should be correctives—real and effective safeguards—against the propensity of any system of theology to violate either "the livingness of reality" or the livingness of the gospel. Had Tillich defined too precisely the human questions to which Christian theology had to supply answers, as regularly happens with confessional catechisms and less nuanced systems of theology (perhaps even Schleiermacher's), his system would at best have dated itself. Some of his critics would say that it is dated, in any case, because in his enucleation of the questions he is too dependent upon existentialism. But because his basic assumption is not that certain specific questions will always be asked, but that the human *qua* human exists as a being who questions, he is able to leave the specific, verbalized questions of successive generations to history, for he recognizes that these, while perennially reflective of the great issues of being, meaning, and the good, will be always thoroughly conditioned by unpredictable contextual factors.

For that reason, especially in his *The Courage to Be,* Tillich shows that different historical epochs have evoked different expressions of the fundamental human anxiety from which our existential questions flow, and that, therefore, theological responses

belonging to one age (let us say the Middle Ages, with their special "anxiety of guilt and condemnation") cannot be applied forth-
with to another age (let us say the contemporary period, which he
considers to be fixated on "the anxiety of meaninglessness and
despair").

In short, the fundamental corrective in Tillich's very coherent
system, preventing it from becoming a *closed* system, is the pole
that he calls "the human situation." For a "Systematiker," he takes
history very seriously, and it is perhaps not accidental that throughout much of his American career he combined the teaching of systematic theology with the history of Christian thought. He knew
very well that "the human situation," from which the *form* though
not the *content* of the theological answer has to be derived, is forever changing, and that for this reason not only the analysis of the
human and worldly condition but also the church's articulation of
gospel must be a responding science, constantly in a state of self-
correction. In this, too, he echoes some of the Protestant wisdom of
Barth—the Barth who was unwilling to be numbered among the
Barthians. Indeed, if anything, Tillich's system is even less sus-
ceptible to closure than is Barth's, for that constantly changing
dimension of it upon which so much depends, namely, "the situation," defies both predictability and ultimate classification. So we
should not be surprised that the first sentences of his introduction
to the first volume of *Systematic Theology* read as follows:

> Theology, as a function of the Christian church, must serve the
> needs of the church. A theological system is supposed to satisfy
> two basic needs: the statement of the truth of the Christian mes-
> sage and the interpretation of this truth for every new genera-
> tion. Theology moves back and forth between the two poles, the
> eternal truth of its foundation and the temporal situation, in
> which the eternal truth must be received.[19]

The requirement that theology must live between tradition and
situation, probing the tradition from the perspective of the present
and impending future, and viewing the human situation through
the lens of what has been "handed over" [*tradere*], has been the

driving impulse toward what some of us have come to call "contextuality" in theology. As I have said in the first volume of my *Christian Theology in a North American Context,* the only thing that I find lacking in Tillich's existential-situational articulation of the Christian faith is a consciousness of *place*: he remained very much a European.[20] But over against the contemporary habit of using the concept of context to define loci in ways that are lacking in both historical consciousness and ecumenicity, I am very glad to be instructed still by his breadth and depth of worldly awareness.

The second emphasis that caused me to doubt my doubts about Tillich's system is expressed most clearly in the introduction to volume 1 of *Systematic Theology.* Here once again Tillich tries to quell the anxieties of those of his critics who fear that the system is a cut-and-dried affair, with predictable religious answers given to predictable human questions. In the "method of correlation," he reminds us,

> question and answer are independent of each other, since it is impossible to derive the answer from the question or the question from the answer. The existential question, namely, man himself in the conflicts of his existential situation, is not the source for the revelatory answer formulated by theology. One cannot derive the divine self-manifestation from an analysis of the human predicament. God speaks to the human situation, against it, and for it. Theological supernaturalism, as represented, for example, by contemporary neo-orthodox theology [read, Karl Barth], is right in asserting the inability of man to reach God under his own power. Man is the question, not the answer. It is equally wrong to derive the question implied in human existence from the revelatory answer. This is impossible because the revelatory answer is meaningless if there is no question to which it is the answer.[21]

This must be appreciated as a very significant methodological statement. It means that, for Tillich, *both* an a priori theology *and* an a priori anthropology are to be spurned. The only way of avoiding the dilemma posed by this situation is for the theologian or the theological community continuously to move between situation and message—and to do so not just intellectually but in a full and personal *participation* in both:

> In order to [formulate the question, the theologian] must participate in the human predicament, not only actually—as he always does—but also in conscious identification. He must participate in man's finitude, which is also his own, and in its anxiety as though he had never received the revelatory answer of "eternity." He must participate in man's estrangement, which is also his own, and show the anxiety of guilt as though he had never received the revelatory answer of "forgiveness." *The theologian does not rest on the theological answer which he announces. He can give it in a convincing way only if he participates with his whole being in the situation of the question, namely, the human predicament. In the light of this demand, the method of correlation protects the theologian from the arrogant claim of having revelatory answers at his disposal. In formulating the answer, he must struggle for it.*[22]

I confess to finding this one of the most poignant descriptions of the task and privilege of Christian theology known to me. It must not be read too quickly, because then one may miss the point that what is involved in this work is a kind of ongoing baptism, like the "continuing baptism" spoken of by the Reformers—or perhaps the symbol of crucifixion would be more appropriate (in any case it is implied in the baptismal reference). What the author is telling us (and there is no doubt that he is speaking autobiographically!) is precisely what Luther told us in his famous sentence *Vivendo, immo moriendo et damnando fit theologus, non intelligendo, legendo aut speculando* (It is by living—nay, rather, by dying and being damned—that a theologian is made, not by understanding, reading, or speculating).[23] Far from being a merely intellectual exercise, a series of questions and answers, theology when it is authentic thrusts its *professor* into an ongoing personal "struggle" of sometimes epic proportions. Such a one may indeed manage to produce a very respectable and well-considered system—is, in fact, under some obligation to do so. But he or she will not be deluded by this accomplishment into thinking that the struggle is finished. For the more one understands of this fullness, the more one knows how little one understands of it. How much more there is to understand, always! Besides, there is . . . tomorrow, the next generation, the next century—the always new and usually unanticipated turnings and shadings of existence called the future.

Above all there is that recurring doubt that dogs the footsteps of genuine faith—like the *Anfechtungen* of Tillich's forebear Martin Luther: the seasons of total abandonment, the dark nights of the soul. As we have already heard from the young Tillich, doubt is not to be excluded, nor is the doubter. Doubt is the negative that serves the positive—and it can *only* serve the positive, ultimately, though in the meantime it can create a hell on earth. It is nevertheless essential to faith, for otherwise faith too easily devolves into credulity, not to say pious presumption. If faith is to be dynamic (and otherwise it would not be faith), *and* if it is to communicate with a doubting world, it must include the possibility of doubt within itself:

> One could call it the existential doubt. . . . [It] is not a permanent experience within the act of faith. But it is always present as an element in the structure of faith. This is the difference between faith and immediate evidence either of perceptual or of logical character. There is no faith without an intrinsic "in spite of" and the courageous affirmation of oneself in the state of ultimate concern.[24]

In conclusion, let me summarize my argument by responding straightforwardly to the question posed at the outset, "How in an age that is increasingly skeptical of all unified systems, since they so regularly turn into ideologies that mask bids for power, is one to maintain the theological pursuit of the unity of truth? Are there ways of ensuring that systematic expressions of Christian teaching may discourage co-optation by power and sustain openness, both to the mystery that refuses to give itself fully to any attempt at comprehension and to other expressions of that mystery?"

Paul Tillich's response to this contemporary concern would seem to be as follows: To begin with, there is no acceptable alternative to a theology that attempts to be orderly, reasonable, and in short systematic. A community that does not continue to work at such an expression of what it professes, which means in practice both giving this task to those specially called to it and engaging in theological discourse throughout the membership, will not survive—and more particularly so, when its survival is no longer guaranteed by extraneous cultural factors.

Yet the danger of oppressive, imposed, "heteronomous" systems *is* real, and the history of Christian theology—not in its greatest exponents (whose greatness is bound up precisely with their knowledge of this) but as employed by powerful ecclesiastical and secular forces—shows that theology as such is not immune to this danger. For this reason three correctives must be present in the work of systematization: First, a historical-contextual corrective: since theology intends to engage specific situations, it must be conscious of, and subject itself to, the always-changing historical context, and therefore permanence of any explicit articulation of religious truth is precluded. Second, an existential corrective: the theologian cannot understand and communicate the Christian message unless he or she undergoes an act of continuous *metanoia,* gaining insight and wisdom only through the loss of accumulated answers and seeming certitude; and therefore the *securitas* of the theoretician is denied the theologian. Third, a spiritual corrective: the satisfaction that comes with understanding is constantly countered not only by the knowledge that one does not know but also by the doubt that questions what is believed true; and therefore the satisfaction of comprehension is prevented from giving way to smugness and what Reinhold Niebuhr called "the menace of finality."

In a manner that greatly baffled the young student that I used to be, our teacher Tillich frequently spoke of the "courage" of intellectual undertakings like those of Augustine or Abelard—even, on occasion, of Karl Barth! This puzzled me and my youthful North American classmates, for we were conditioned to think that courage applied only to deeds. I now know better. Those who really try to understand the whole, knowing not only that the Ultimate, while it grasps us, cannot be grasped *by* us, but that there are dangers attendant upon the very exercise of such understanding that must be guarded against: such persons, when they attempt the thing anyway, must be called men and women of courage. Tillich's remembered voice still calls us to strive for the courage of holistic, integrated, and (yes!) systematic thinking.

3 Reinhold Niebuhr
An American Theology of the Tragic— and Beyond

Paul Tillich, a refugee in 1933 from the violence that great lies about the human condition inevitably beget, insisted upon truth telling as the vocation of genuine faith. His most popular book, *The Courage to Be,* takes its title from the German expression *Mut zum Leben.* But for Tillich the courage to *be,* that is, the courage to affirm and embrace life despite its perils, is inseparable from the pursuit of truth. It is easy to affirm existence if one can blot out the knowledge of all that negates it. The only kind of courage in which faith is interested is the courage that is given those who open themselves to all aspects of creaturely life, including death, the apparently final negation of life. *Mut zum Leben,* the courage to be, is inseparable from *Mut zur Wahrheit*—the courage to be truthful.[1]

Those who confess with John that *Jesus Christ* is "the Truth" (John 14:16) dare not imagine that they are in possession of the truth. The whole language of possession is inappropriate to this tradition, and nowhere more so than in connection with "the truth." But it is possible to be *oriented toward truth,* and this kind of truth orientation [*Wahrheitsorientierung*] is the vocation of the community of witness to the Christ. It is the Christian's heritage from the prophetic tradition of our parental faith. Whoever is grasped by it can never be satisfied with other kinds of orientation to which religious people are commonly given, such as orientation to comfort, or piety, or happiness, or even personal salvation.

The subject of this chapter was such a one.

The truth to which Reinhold Niebuhr exposed himself and sought to expose his contemporaries was a truth that neither his society nor the churches within it could receive with equanimity. Niebuhr had to share the fate of prophets throughout the ages because he would not assume the role of the false prophet and tell his listeners what they wished to hear. While Niebuhr today has his supporters (though, interestingly, he did not found a school), one has the impression that his most basic ideas are still alien to his homeland. As continued reference to his name in both religious and secular outlets attests, the "voice" of Reinhold Niebuhr still echoes in our ears, yet his "words"—many of them—are profoundly neglected.

Among the forgotten words of Reinhold Niebuhr is the word I have highlighted in the title of this chapter: "tragic." It is perhaps inevitable that of all the key words associated with Niebuhrian analysis—paradox, ambiguity, proximate goals, irony, impossible possibility, and so on—the word "tragedy" would have been the most vulnerable where public memory is concerned. Tragedy is not a concept that suits our North American outlook—which may explain why we so often trivialize it by associating it with external events. In his play *Soldiers,* the German author Rolf Hochhuth has one of his characters remark that in America the word "tragedy" does not exist; "they call it migraine."[2] Another author writes that the bourgeois think that "tragedy is . . . an unpleasantness which might have been avoided by better social arrangements and an improved technology."[3] The vision upon which our so-called New World was built, and which from the eighteenth century onward it elaborated in increasingly exaggerated terms, eliminated both the concepts with which the idea of the tragic is bound up: the concept of an irrevocable link with a tangled and guilty past, and the concept of the inseparability of good and evil in human behavior. It was believed—it became, indeed, the cornerstone of our belief system—that, freed from the cycle of injustice and revenge characteristic of the Old World, human beings could at last accentuate the positive, eliminate the negative, and have done with "the ambiguities of history." This vast and *almost*-unpeopled continent would be a "new Eden" for the "new Adam."[4] Tragedy was a word applicable, perhaps, to European history, but not to America.

It would be an understatement to say that Reinhold Niebuhr did not agree with this outlook. It would be truer to say that his entire witness—his "ministry," as he himself continued to think of his professional life[5]—was devoted to the exposition not only of the naïveté of this highly positive view but of its implicit and explicit dangers both to those who imbibed it and to those in proximity to the nation that imbibed it, who must suffer the consequences of such self-deception. For in his view the American Dream, while admirable and even noble as a modest vision entertained by the exploited and expelled masses, had become, in the hands of modernity's ideologues and powerful classes, an ironclad ideology: an ideology ultimately more insidious, perhaps, than the more clear-cut and militant ideology of Marxism-Leninism, its estranged cousin, precisely because the free-enterprise version of modernity could seem so attractive. Besides, the measure of visible success achieved by a people under the spell of this dream could conveniently mitigate its false assumptions and camouflage its darker consequences.

"Man's story is not a success story." That was the caption under the portrait of Reinhold Niebuhr, set against the backdrop of a turbulent, stormy landscape with (very insightfully on the part of the artist) a cross on the horizon, that appeared on the cover of *Time* magazine's twenty-fifth anniversary issue. That such a portrait and such a caption should be thought worthy of such an occasion, and in the spring of 1948, while America and the West were still basking in the heady success of victory in war, created some rather predictable shock waves in our society fifty years ago, not least of all among church folk.

Would it shock us still? That is a deceptively tricky question, and part of the trick involved in it lies in the fact that it is hard for us to imagine a time in which *Time* magazine featured mainline Protestant theologians on its cover! It says a great deal about the metamorphosis of Christendom that has been occurring, silently but surely, over the past several decades, that in the first half of this century—but not the second—not only Niebuhr but most of the serious Protestant thinkers of the age made their appearances on the cover of *Time* and other popular journals. One wonders: has part of the reason why mainline Protestantism has become sideline Protestantism to do with the fact that its witness is so internalized, so in-house, so preoccupied with its own interior problems and survival? Or is its *Mut zur Wahrheit* so wan and timid, or perhaps so confined to the more conspicuous ethical questions, that it would not dare such sweeping judgments as that "Man's story is not a success story"?

Be that as it may, the sentence appearing on *Time's* silver jubilee cover is a remarkable summary of *part* of the message of Reinhold Niebuhr's "ministry"—an *essential* part: the negative witness without which the positive would be rendered innocuous; the critical theology without which any attempt at foundational theology would be little more than a predictable orthodoxy, whether liberal or conservative; the deconstruction without which reconstruction could, as such, not even occur. Reinhold Niebuhr's theology (and I do not hesitate for a moment to speak of this *theology!*) is confessional and not merely professional theology because it accurately identifies the point of real conflict between the gospel and the *Zeitgeist* of the context in which gospel is to be proclaimed. It belongs to the proclamation of good news that it must seek out and do battle with the bad news indigenous to its context. Gospel truth is truth that is revealed only in an open struggle with untruth. Where that struggle is avoided in favor of a more placid type of religion (and is not our cultural Protestantism just a name for this avoidance?), the Christian message is reduced to slogans and platitudes, some of which may retain some vestige of faith's profession but none of which is able to make the breakthrough into confession. The Barmen Declaration was a *confession* of the faith chiefly because it was not satisfied with its highly positive and impeccably orthodox statement of the lordship of Jesus Christ but had to make quite explicit, in its *damnamus*, the falsehood that was revealed as such in the light of Christ's sovereignty: "Jesus Christ

. . . is the one Word of God . . . which we have to trust and obey in life and in death"; therefore *"[w]e reject the false doctrine,* as though the Church could and would have to acknowledge . . . other events and powers, figures and truths, as God's revelation."[6]

Reinhold Niebuhr's testimony to the falseness of the "success story" entertained by the dominant culture of his society is the *damnamus* of his Christian confession of faith. And if his theology is heavily weighted on the side of this negative witness; if he did not, like the middle and later Barth, move decisively from the via negativa to the via positiva; if, unlike his colleague Tillich, he did not produce a complete system of theology but continued throughout his life to ponder the flawed character of the human condition and to comment at length upon the historical particularities of his period, it is surely because, *given* his societal context, there was no real alternative for one grasped by the divine impulse and necessity of truth telling. For it is one thing to announce, as Barmen did, that the sovereignty of Jesus Christ precludes loyalty to a rank fascist ideology, and something else to proclaim that the message of "Jesus Christ and him crucified" entails a judgment upon all human success stories, even one that had accumulated for itself so much seeming evidence as the American Dream had laid up by 1948.

Yet it would be entirely misleading to think (as some actually do think) that Niebuhr's witness was one of negation only. In his lifetime, he was frequently branded "a pessimist," and the epithet follows him to this day. But this assessment, which can be and is made also of Augustine, Calvin, and the entire classical Protestant tradition, is the judgment of little minds for whom the facile alternatives of optimism and pessimism are substitutes for more mature categories of analysis. The fact that Niebuhr could be so quickly labeled by many of his fellow Americans indicates more about America than it does about Niebuhr. More importantly, the fact that many of those who accused Niebuhr of pessimism were Christians indicates how poorly Christianity on this continent has grasped what he correctly identified as "the Jewish-Christian alternative" to *both* optimistic and pessimistic views of historical existence. Niebuhr expressed that "alternative" in the following way:

> In this view, human life is meaningful even though its existence in a world of nature, which is not completely sympathetic to the human enterprise, is not fully explained. The world of nature is not completely interpreted in terms of human values or ideals, as in naive naturalism, nor is it simply a dark abyss or a "trampling march of unconscious power" which man defies and against which he rebels. Man and nature are reconciled by faith in a center and source of meaning which transcends both man and nature.[7]

As with Augustine and Luther, from both of whom Niebuhr learned much of his theology, the Source of meaning that delivers Niebuhr's humanity from pessimism and tames the "cynicism" that he knew even as a young pastor is located beyond the historical process. And just this is the great offence of Niebuhr so far as the *modern* appropriation of the optimistic worldview is concerned. For modernity, as distinct from both of the founding traditions of Western civilization (Jerusalem and Athens), insists that the principle of meaning and salvation is built into the historical process itself. From the perspective of modernity's faith in progress—the faith that my late countryman George P. Grant claimed is the real "religion" of North America—Reinhold Niebuhr's unforgivable sin was nothing more nor less than his dogged adherence to the traditions of biblical faith. For modernity could only hear of the necessity of a redemption from beyond historical cause and effect as a pessimistic credo. But Niebuhr knew, long before it was known to most of his contemporaries, that modernity had precisely in this sense run its course:

> While modern optimism was in its prime it could sneer at the pessimism of historic religion because the illusions of the former prevented it from recognizing the tragic realities of life and history which the latter had incorporated into its universe of meaning. Now that these illusions have been dispelled, it is pos-

sible to recognize again that historic religion has a note of provisional pessimism in its optimism, for the simple reason that it takes cognizance of more of the facts of human existence.[8]

The only flaw in this statement, I think, is its too confident belief that " these illusions have been dispelled." Today, it seems to me, one may rightly say that the overt and in a way even spontaneous optimism of the Enlightenment has been profoundly judged by the most memorable events of the twentieth century, so that in its purest forms it is not an option for thinking people. But that does not mean that its "illusions" are "dispelled." They may be dispelled, or at least severely curtailed, for those who lack either the material or the spiritual insulation needed to go on living as if (in Martin Buber's words) "it would grow ever lighter." But many in our midst do still possess such insulation; and, moreover, powerful ideologies in their decline and demise beget contrived and militant versions of themselves, which are more obstinate than the originals.

Twenty-five years ago, in a book that certainly expressed a Niebuhrian perspective, I made use of an expression that I learned from Sydney Hook: "our national philosophy of optimism."[9] The "official optimism" of postwar North America is not the real thing. It is an imitative and defensive optimism, which must be nourished constantly and protected from truth that calls it into question and challenges its very foundations. Having no operative frame of reference for the experience of negation, a public reared on its own success story, endlessly rehearsed, demands of its leadership, its educational institutions, its entertainment industry that they provide, if not direct reinforcement of its will to believe in itself, at least sufficient diversion to stave off its temptation to disbelief and cynicism. (Appallingly, the diversion provided is not infrequently war.)

Above all, such a public will make such demands of its religions—will in fact become in some new sense a "religious" public, creating for itself new religions if the old ones cannot be molded to fit its repressive needs. Unfortunately, the old religions in North America have shown themselves more than willing to supply this demand, or to attempt it. Whether in conservative or liberal or even self-styled radical versions, Christianity on this continent today has set for itself the overall program of yet another phase of positive religion. The churches that have success stories to tell today—churches mainly of the Christian Right, but also the megachurches and media-conscious congregations of moderate and liberal North American Christianity—are those that have been able to capitalize on the insecurity of middle-class "future shock" and find persuasive ways of retrieving the security and alleged happiness of our rhetorical past. Meanwhile, the more conventional denominations, the remnants of classical Protestantism, whose "qualified optimism" (Niebuhr) is insufficiently slick and sloganizable to appeal to this same demand for a return to positive "spirituality," have not yet shown themselves capable of the deeper wisdom that Niebuhr expressed in his appropriation of the concept of the tragic.

Niebuhr concluded the essay from which I have been quoting here— "Optimism, Pessimism and Religious Faith"—with a paragraph that contains in miniature his understanding of tragedy in relation to Christian belief:

> [For faith] the mystery of life is comprehended in meaning, though no human statement of the meaning can fully resolve the mystery. *The tragedy of life is recognized, but faith prevents tragedy from being pure tragedy.* Perplexity remains, but there is no perplexity unto despair. Evil is neither accepted as inevitable nor regarded as a proof of the meaninglessness of life. Gratitude and contrition are mingled, which means that life is both appreciated and challenged. To such faith the generations are bound to return after they have pursued the mirages in the desert to which they are tempted from time to time by the illusions of particular eras.[10]

The Christian faith, then, recognizes the tragedy that life under the conditions of historical existence entails; but as faith in a God whose will for the life of the creation transcends the tragic experience of the creature, Christian faith is prevented from embracing "pure tragedy." This thesis was developed by Niebuhr in many places, but most fully in his 1937 collection of essays on the Christian interpretation of history, bearing the title *Beyond Tragedy*.[11] Interestingly enough, this work was reissued by Niebuhr nearly thirty years later (in 1965), without any attempt at updating, apart from the prefatory note indicating that while, as a work written prior to World War II, it contained references that were now "dated," "the meaning is obvious and the substance of the points illustrated is not affected."[12] Obviously, Niebuhr felt a particular commitment to the position he had taken in this book, and this despite (or perhaps somewhat because of?) the fact that it had been harshly criticized by many reviewers and, more painfully, by some of his close associates.[13] Perhaps he felt that by 1965 the position he had taken in these sermonic essays would be more immediately accessible than it had been in 1937; and surely, for a significant minority of North American Christians, that was the case. For the vast majority, however, his thesis was as hard to swallow in 1965 as it had been in 1937.

The connecting thought that binds the quite diverse essays of this book together is expressed in its clearest terms in the preface:

> It is the thesis of these essays that the Christian view of history passes through the sense of the tragic to a hope and an assurance which is "beyond tragedy." The cross, which stands at the centre of the Christian worldview, reveals both the seriousness of human sin and the purpose and power of God to overcome it. It reveals man violating the will of God in his highest moral and spiritual achievements (in Roman law and Jewish religion) and God absorbing this evil into Himself in the very moment of its most vivid expression. Christianity's view of history is tragic insofar as it recognizes evil as an inevitable concomitant of even the highest spiritual enterprises. It is beyond tragedy insofar as it does not regard evil as inherent in existence itself but as finally under the dominion of a good God.[14]

The cornerstone of the position taken by Niebuhr in this work — and in most of his other writings as well — is located in that one sentence beginning, significantly, with the words, "The cross . . ."

Contrary to those (including, in some of their judgments, both Barth and Tillich) who tend to relegate Niebuhr's work to Christian anthropology, Niebuhr's anthropology, as well as his theology, ecclesiology, and eschatology, is grounded in his Christology—or, as with Wilhelm Pauck we might say more accurately, his "picture of Christ." The fact that he did not develop a Christology in the usual systematic form does not mean that he did not have one. His "picture of Christ," like that of Luther (also an unsystematic theologian), accentuates the soteriological dimension of Christology, and in this he is a thoroughly Western and a thoroughly Protestant thinker—though he himself would have said "biblical," for he did not find in the New Testament anything like the kind of independent substantialistic interest in the "person" of Christ that came to dominate early christological doctrine. His christological roots are Pauline and Lutheran; in fact, as I have argued elsewhere,[15] there is in Niebuhr's work as a whole an original but absolutely authentic articulation of that spirit and method of theology that Luther named *theologia crucis,* and this despite the fact that Niebuhr nowhere (to my knowledge) uses that terminology.

It is certainly the crucified Christ that draws his particular interest, indeed his faith; he does not allow the "event of the third day" to distract his attention away from Good Friday. On the contrary, the function of the resurrection and of the advent of the divine Spirit in his thought, as in that of Käsemann, Moltmann, Sölle, Kitamori, Koyama, and others, is precisely to evoke in human beings *the faith* that is needed if one is to see the cross for what it is, namely as the revelation of both the impossibility of the human condition and the new possibility that is given despite it and through it. For the "meaning" that faith clings to in the midst of life's incongruities is most concretely expressed in that "mystery": "The cross, which stands at the centre of the Christian worldview, reveals both the seriousness of human sin and the purpose and power of God to overcome it."[16]

What Niebuhr often called "the logic of the cross" confronts humanity—ancient humanity with its pessimistic fatalism and modern humanity with its optimistic voluntarism—with the truly tragic character of human existence and history. Human beings in their *being* and not only in their doing are distortions of their calling, their divine vocation and possibility. In Tillichian language (which, however, Niebuhr did not like), our existence is a contradiction of our essence. In individual lives, this contradiction manifests itself in ways that are more properly called pathetic; only in a few human beings is self-knowledge elevated to the heights of the tragic. Most of us are Willy Lomans, not King Lears—or even Hamlets! Yet considered as a species, our condition is tragic, because our sin is not only private but corporate, altering (as we may say very concretely today) the entire created order. To the horror of his liberal contemporaries, Niebuhr revived the idea of original sin, and in the process redeemed it—for many of us—from its Babylonian captivity to quasi-sexual and organic misconceptions by relating it, as Tillich did, to the dimension of tragedy.

This recognition of "the tragic dimension" of the biblical concept of sin made it possible for Niebuhr to recognize a lasting link between Jerusalem and Athens. Though he was generally critical of "Greek" thought, and in the tradition of high liberalism saw it as a kind of betrayal of early Christianity, much to the consternation of Tillich,[17] he found in the Greek *tragedians* a continuity with the tradition of Jerusalem—and one that was accentuated by the contrast of both Athens and Jerusalem with modernity:

> However wide and deep the differences which separate the Christian view of life from that of Greek tragedy, it must be apparent that there are greater similarities between the two than between either and the utilitarian rationalism which has dominated contemporary culture. Both measure life in the same depth; and neither gives itself to the simple delusion that the titanic forces of human existence, whether they spring from below the level of consciousness or rise above the level of human limitations, can easily be brought under the control of some little scheme of prudent rationality.[18]

The cross of Jesus Christ reveals the tragic character of human existence and history. The human situation is tragic, and not merely pathetic; so that even in this dimension of its revealing truth the cross is in some sense enabling, as is the tragic vision in Greek drama, in Shakespeare's tragedies, and to some extent in Ibsen and modern tragedians. But the illumination that accompanies Golgotha's "darkness at noon" does not rest in the awareness of our tragic condition. "[T]he basic message of Christian faith is a message of *hope in tragedy*."[19]

> [The message of the cross] declares that when the Christ, by whom the world was made, enters the world, the world will not receive him. "He came unto his own and his own received him not." Human existence denies its own deepest and most essential nature. That is tragic. But when that fact is understood, when men cease to make the standards of a sinful existence the norms of life but accept its true norm, even though they fail to obey it, their very contribution opens the eyes of faith. This is the Godly sorrow that worketh repentance. Out of this despair hope is born. The hope is simply this: that the contradictions of human existence, which man cannot surmount, are swallowed up in the life of God Himself. The God of Christian faith is not only creator but redeemer. He does not allow human existence to end tragically. He snatches victory from defeat. He is Himself defeated in history but He is also victorious in that defeat.[20]

Some lament the fact that Niebuhr did not develop more fully (by which most seem to mean more doctrinally) this hope that is "beyond tragedy." In fact, however—and I mean in the actual daily work and witness of his life, his "ministry"—he did develop it, and in very concrete terms: for what could be more redolent of real as distinct from rhetorical hope than the thousands of articles, commentaries on current events, sermons, speeches, and public dialogues in which Reinhold Niebuhr tried nearly every day of his life to inculcate in his hearers the spirit of hope? This included hope for change in the midst of seemingly irrevocable forces of historical destiny; hope for the achievement of "proximate goals" despite the unreachability of perfection; hope for *metanoia* in a people—America; the West—whose ironic and tragic reality is so inextricably bound up with its finest achievements; hope for life in the kingdoms of death.[21] Many of his students, to be sure, only heard him speaking about "the ambiguities of history"; they did not follow him in his lifetime awareness that Christians do not rest in these ambiguities but (as his famous so-called serenity prayer insists) seek to "change what can be changed."

But there is another reason why Reinhold Niebuhr did not elaborate in a more consistent and theoretical way the side of his position that is "beyond tragedy," and that is the reason that we recalled at the outset of this chapter: that he was captive to the vocation of truth. Truth demands not only to be told but to be heard. Niebuhr knew that the truth to which he must continuously direct his fellow citizens, and especially the Christians among them, was the first dimension of this illumination: the reality of life's tragic character. How can a people dedicated to the pursuit of happiness hear *that* truth—and from a source, the Christian church, to which it looks for assurance of the legitimacy of such a pursuit? Niebuhr understood very well that what America expected to hear from its religious leadership, whether conservative or liberal, was a message of triumph—without dwelling long or deeply upon the realities of that over which the triumph occurs. Early in his professional career, while still a pastor in Detroit, he penned some thoughts that, I suspect, he did not find it necessary to revise throughout his relatively long life. Commenting on a sermon he had preached on Paul's "We preach Christ crucified" (1 Cor. 1:23), he wrote:

> I don't think I ever felt greater joy in preaching a sermon. . . . Now I see [the cross] as a symbol of ultimate reality. . . . It seems pathetic to me that liberalism has too little appreciation of the tragedy of life to understand the cross and orthodoxy insists too much upon the absolute uniqueness of the sacrifice of Christ to make the preaching of the cross effective.[22]

In a similar vein, in a sentence that parallels almost exactly the twenty-first thesis of Luther's Heidelberg Disputation,[23] Niebuhr felt impelled to conclude: "Most profoundly the atonement of

Christ is a revelation of what life actually is."[24] Niebuhr's so-called Christian Realism is not the hard-nosed, half-pagan propensity to affirm the status quo that it is sometimes made out to be. It is in the tradition of the *theologia crucis,* which would rather be true to what "actually is" than to produce beautiful theories of salvation at the expense of reality. On that score, Niebuhr would have agreed with the French philosopher who quipped, "Theory is fine, but it doesn't prevent things from existing."[25]

More importantly, positive and pious doctrinal affirmations of hope uttered in a context where the existential despair they are intended to engage is thoroughly and successfully repressed can only contribute to their continued repression. If the resurrection—or rather, as I call it, resurrectionism—has dominated in the piety of North American Protestants, it has been due to the need of our "official optimism" for a plain and straightforward symbol of triumph. If we retained the cross, it had to be an empty cross. And in the end it has proven all too empty.

In her provocative study *Tragic Vision and Divine Compassion,* Wendy Farley charges that Christianity, at least as we have practiced it, is inept in its handling of the tragic. I am in complete agreement with her. So, I believe, would Reinhold Niebuhr have been (and it is curious that she does not cite him more than once in the entire book). While Christian piety on this continent has been busy demonstrating faith's triumph over all that negates, daily life in this once–New World of ours has been taking on, increasingly, the tragic dimensions that were and still are present in the old worlds from which we have all come hither. In our collective past, some of us knew something about those tragic dimensions: our seventeenth- and eighteenth-century ancestors, if they were poor and marginalized people (as most of them were), knew them; our African ancestors knew them; our more recent fellow citizens from Asia and Latin America knew and know them.

And our best authors and artists have known them. The following words were penned by one of them. They could almost have been written by Reinhold Niebuhr:

> Life is made up of marble and mud. And, without all the deeper trust in a comprehensive sympathy above us, we might hence be led to suspect the insult of a sneer, as well as an immitigable frown, on the iron countenance of fate. What is called poetic insight is the gift of discerning, in this sphere of strangely mingled elements, the beauty and the majesty which are compelled to assume a garb so sordid.[26]

There is indeed an innate knowledge of this tragic dimension in the heart of every thinking person, though it may surface more as pathos than as tragedy. But we have been "beguiled by what is good in human existence" and by the rhetoric of modernity "into a false optimism."[27] And therefore we miss not only the mud but also the marble, not only the misery but also the grandeur of the life for which the gospel of the crucified one liberates us.

Yet with the demise of modernity and its religion of progress, this official optimism also fades. Sometimes one has the impression that all that remains is the smile on the face of this Cheshire cat—the rhetoric that must be dragged out of our archives by every new president, every successful minister, every advertiser. The future of Protestantism on this continent—and I mean Protestantism in its classical sense—depends upon our reclaiming this biblical familiarity with human tragedy that is at the heart of our Christian story and, with increasing clarity, the heart of our society. The gospel points us "beyond tragedy," but only by first making us more profoundly conscious of that beyond which it would direct our gaze.

It will be appropriate to close, as I began, with a quotation from Paul Tillich—one which shows the extent to which, despite their differences, these two longtime colleagues were heirs to the same traditions of wisdom:

> History shows that, over and over again, as though by a logic of tragedy, the achievements of man turn against man himself.

This was true of the great creative achievements of sacramental faith as well as the achievements of technical reason. Therefore the Christian message cannot anticipate a future situation devoid of tragedy even if the demonic forces in the present situation can be conquered. The authentic Christian message is never utopian, whether through belief in progress or through faith in revolution.[28]

4 Dietrich Bonhoeffer
Discipleship as World Commitment

For reasons broached in the Preface and elaborated in the Introduction, I have intentionally approached this material in a personal
way. In the case of Bonhoeffer, the approach will have to be even
more personal—and this despite the fact that, of the four theologians treated so far, he is the only one I never met.

It was the summer of 1949. I had returned to my parental home
in a southwestern Ontario village from the city of Toronto, where
I had been studying music at the Royal Conservatory. During that
year in Toronto, I had heard something that I have since found is
extremely rare: Christian preaching in the classical Protestant
mode—intelligent yet not merely rationalistic preaching; literary,
biblically based sermons that engaged one's whole person in a profound yet entirely unsentimental way. Under their impact and a
young lifetime of struggling with God and the world, I found myself moving from music to theology—a transition that Martin
Luther would have thought a very natural one, though at the time
it did not seem so to me. At age twenty-one I determined to enter
the Christian ministry, and I returned to my village home to work
for the summer and to try as best I could to prepare myself for university, a prospect that I had never before entertained.

I had read through most of Shakespeare's plays and three fascinating biographies of Luther when, one day, there appeared in
the post a small package from the preacher of those thoughtful
sermons. It was the first edition in English of Dietrich Bonhoeffer's *The Cost of Discipleship,* which had come out during the
previous year, 1948.[1] I had never heard of Dietrich Bonhoeffer—

hardly anybody in the English-speaking world had. The war had ended only four years earlier, and even the writings of Barth, Tillich, and Niebuhr were still new to most North Americans. I am probably one of the few extant working theologians who began to read Bonhoeffer without the slightest notion of who he had been, and (what is more significant, I think, as I shall try to say presently) without any sort of *pre*-understanding of what I would hear from him.

At first, I was puzzled by his book. It would require several years of reading theology and becoming personally acquainted with Bonhoeffer's Germany before I could understand why the book perplexed me. I can say now that it had to do with contexts — a later preoccupation of mine. Bonhoeffer's context, at least spiritually speaking, was almost 180 degrees removed from mine. What had brought about my disenchantment with the Christianity prevalent in my village church and society as it was then (it is not so today — but that is another story) was precisely the kind of strict attention to moral rectitude that I now, quite erroneously, heard Bonhoeffer talking about in *The Cost of Discipleship*.[2] What had so attracted me to Luther, on the contrary, a Reformer virtually unheard of in my almost exclusively Anglo-Saxon Protestant milieu, was precisely his emphasis upon justification by grace through faith, "not by works, lest anyone should boast"! And here was Dietrich Bonhoeffer accentuating "works" again, and "the *cost* of discipleship." I felt a certain wariness in the presence of this message. Did my preacher friend in Toronto, who sent me the book, want to deliver me back into the dour and unforgiving fold of this works-righteousness religion, the moralism of which was matched only by its hypocrisy — its unfounded boasting?

I still had to learn, of course, that there is no nondangerous theology; that theology *has* to be dialectical, because otherwise one side of the story will obscure the other side, and one will end up with some flagrant heresy — if not legalism then antinomianism; if not rationalism then fideism, and so forth. As I have told my students in recent years: In theology you have to keep talking or else somebody will believe your last sentence. To use Reformation language, I had been reared on a religion of law without gospel, and Dietrich Bonhoeffer—in that so-very-Lutheran Germany (that knew only one side of Luther)—had been reared on gospel without law; or, as he himself put it, on grace as a principle, a pronouncement, a *fait accompli*: "cheap grace." "The essence of grace, we suppose," he wrote, "is that the account has been paid in advance; and, because it has been paid, everything can be had for nothing. . . . Grace alone does everything, they say, and so everything can remain as it was before."[3]

Thus do contexts alter meanings. To understand Dietrich Bonhoeffer aright (and the same thing can be said, *mutatis mutandis,* of Paul, or Augustine, or Hildegaard of Bingen, and countless others) I had to learn about a whole culture that was very different from my own—far more different then than now, perhaps. And this is a lesson that is still regularly ignored, or is wholly unsuspected, by North Americans, who tend to be consumers in theology as in all other things, and go about the world with our shopping carts looking for interesting, marketable religious ideas that are the results of other peoples' pain. Dietrich Bonhoeffer, like many Latin American and other Christians from whom we would later borrow the language of liberation, had paid very dearly for his wisdom, and one could only grasp it for the wisdom that it was by listening to him from the perspective of one who had entered into the pain of one's own society, repressed, concealed, and—withal— "different" as that might be.

While I was in university during the last year of the 1940s and the early 1950s my comprehension of Bonhoeffer improved a little with a greater knowledge of modern European history, and, as his other works began to appear in English and I learned more about Bonhoeffer's life and martyrdom, some of the impact of his thought broke through to me. Still, during the 1950s, even in a place like Union Theological Seminary in New York, where Bonhoeffer had studied briefly, the name of Dietrich Bonhoeffer was rarely heard in the North American context, and, I think, the

Anglo-Saxon world generally. And then, in 1963, the late Bishop John A. T. Robinson published his best-seller, *Honest to God*.[4]

In that little book, which seems to be now so very characteristic of the 1960s, Dietrich Bonhoeffer—or rather, Bishop Robinson's interpretation of him—plays an important role, along with two other continental thinkers, Rudolf Bultmann and Paul Tillich. (Barth, incidentally, is mentioned only twice, rather unfavorably, and Reinhold Niebuhr not at all.) What Robinson wanted to tell us in *Honest to God* is that as modern people, citizens of "the secular city" (another key title of the period, as some will remember), thinking Christians would have to become entirely candid—"honest"—about their incapacity to hold to a good deal of the "thinking, piety and moral attitudes of the conventional Church."[5] The essence of the faith, Robinson believed, could be retained only if we were prepared to discard the outmoded doctrinal and ecclesiastical forms in which it was encased. This was something that liberal theologians had been saying for a hundred years, of course, but now, with the dawning of what was soon styled "the Age of Aquarius," the time was ripe for such a message, apparently, at least among those (as we said) with-it individuals who still associated themselves with the Christian religion.

To help us make this transition into the postreligious world, Bishop Robinson made use of Tillich's "ground of being" conception of God, of Bultmann's program of the dymythologization of scripture, and of Bonhoeffer's "religionless Christianity." At one point in his book, there is a footnote in which the bishop affirms that one really should know something of Bonhoeffer's "previous writings" and names especially his *Life Together*,[6] but *Honest to God* concerns itself only with certain fragments from Bonhoeffer's last writings, collected by Eberhard Bethge under the title *Letters and Papers from Prison* (in the United States, *Prisoner for God*), which would have been the first and smaller edition of this work, translated by Reginald Fuller and published by SCM Press in 1953.

These fragments are by now well known, or (to speak more accurately) the rumor of them is known. That is partly so because, through their publicizing by Bishop Robinson and others, these undeveloped and almost aphoristic thoughts of the imprisoned Bonhoeffer helped to shape the allegedly radical Christianity that began first to make its appearance in the 1960s and is with us in various expressions still today. The fragments achieved, as it were, a life of their own. They are memorialized in three of the chapter headings of Robinson's small book: "The End of Theism?" "The Man for Others," and "Worldly Holiness." Perhaps the most famous passage runs as follows:

> There is no . . . way [back to the land of childhood]—at any rate not if it means deliberately abandoning our mental integrity; the only way is that of Matthew 18:3, i.e., through repentance, through *ultimate* honesty.
> And we cannot be honest unless we recognize that we have to live in the world *etsi deus non daretur*. And this is just what we do recognize—before God! God himself compels us to recognize it. So our coming of age leads us to a true recognition of our situation before God. God would have us know that we must live as men who manage our lives without him. The God who is with us is the God who forsakes us (Mark 15:34). The God who lets us live in the world without the working hypothesis of God is the God before whom we stand continually. Before God and with God we live without God. God lets himself be pushed out of the world on to the cross. He is weak and powerless in the world, and that is precisely the way, the only way, in which he is with us and helps us. Matt. 8:17 makes it quite clear that Christ helps us, not by virtue of his omnipotence, but by virtue of his weakness and suffering.[7]

For many who have approached Bonhoeffer from the hermeneutical perspective of this and the other seemingly novel fragments from the posthumously published *Letters and Papers,* his work represents a radical discontinuity with the tradition. From that vantage point, consequently, it could be erroneous to consider

him under the category "neo-orthodox," even generously interpreted.

That judgment, however understandable it may be in the light of
the history that I have just sketched, seems to me the consequence
of a limited, not to say a very superficial knowledge both of Bonhoeffer and of the others belonging to the so-called neo-orthodox
movement. That movement, as we have already seen with three of
its spokespersons, incorporates a considerable variety of approach
and opinion, including significant disagreements. We should not
expect it to be any more uniform than, for example, Reformation
theology or medieval scholasticism. Perhaps what makes for a
theological movement in any case is not so much a commonality of
answers as a commonality of questions. Bonhoeffer is critical of
Barth's "positivism of revelation"; his language is nothing at all
like the ontological- existential language of Tillich; and his demand
for an articulated theology is much more insistent than Niebuhr's.
Yet they all know that they are living in a post-Christendom world;
they all reject, without wholly dispensing with, the liberalism of the
previous period; and they all return to Reformation and biblical
sources for illumination. (I shall pursue this side of the matter more
systematically in my Conclusions.)

As for Bonhoeffer, what is obscured by the habit of interpreting
him too quickly on the basis of some of the final insights of his
brief life is not only the continuity and (if I may) theo-logicality of
the evolution of his thought but even the deeper theological
grounds and meaning of these late fragments themselves. When
one probes into the fragments in the light of Bonhoeffer's previous thought, one finds, among other things, how closely the concerns he expresses in them relate to those of other representatives
of this movement—especially, in some important ways, Barth: not
the conservative Barth of "the Barthians," but the radical Barth
who did not wish to be a Barthian. For instance, it would be difficult to understand what Bonhoeffer says about "religionless Christianity" (Robinson's special theme) if one knew nothing of Karl
Barth's profound and extensive critique of religion. More signifi-

cantly, it is virtually impossible to understand the highly paradoxical language of the fragments (including the one that I quoted earlier) without having some knowledge of Barth's return to the *christological basis* of the faith. And, perhaps most importantly, as Larry Rasmussen has shown in the final chapter of his study (with Renate Bethge) of Bonhoeffer's significance for North Americans,[8] it would be quite impossible to grasp in any genuine way the radical *ethic* of Bonhoeffer if one had no background understanding of Luther's *theology* of the cross *and* of Bonhoeffer's sense of the betrayal of that theology by the peculiarly Lutheran form of Constantinianism.

In *The Cost of Discipleship,* as we have seen, Bonhoeffer had strong things to say against the sort of theology, masquerading as Reformation doctrine, that contents itself with correct theory ("justification by grace through faith," for instance) and does not express itself in act, in practice—in short, in discipleship. Theology without ethics is not theology in the biblical sense. But the reverse is also true, and he knew it—true, and in the end probably more dangerous. For ethics without any theological foundation, or with only flimsy and mostly assumed or rote theological foundations, will finally beg such questions, and the community governed by this approach will prove indistinguishable from the societal matrix that it hopes to engage.

It is this latter danger that must concern all serious Christians in the North American context, and it was characteristic of the critical acumen of Dietrich Bonhoeffer that he perceived this already in his earliest personal acquaintance with the Christianity on this continent. In a reflective and still-pertinent essay on American Christianity, Bonhoeffer wrote:

> American theology and the American church as a whole have never been able to understand the meaning of "criticism" by the word of God and all that it signifies. Right to the last they do not understand that God's "criticism" touches even religion, the

Christianity of the churches and the sanctification of Christians, and that God has founded his church beyond religion *and beyond ethics.*[9]

Passages like this, with their strong criticism of the identification of Christian faith with religion, certainly cannot be said to be radically discontinuous with the late fragments from prison. More importantly for my present concern, however, is the warning in this particular statement against substituting "ethics" (or perhaps he should have said morality) for the life of faith and the witness of the church. But such a warning would hardly surprise anyone familiar with the characteristic emphases and the evolution of Bonhoeffer's thought.

For his ethic emerges from, constantly returns to, and is wholly dependent upon his theology, and his theology is nothing more nor less than an ongoing, spiritual-intellectual, and above all [his word] "critical" reflection upon the unfolding of the world, including its religion, seen in the light of the gospel of "Jesus Christ and him crucified." While that christological foundation of Bonhoeffer's ethic is present in everything that he wrote, it is perhaps most explicitly developed, as one would expect, in his book *Ethics.*[10] "The point of departure for Christian ethics," he writes.

is not the reality of one's own self, or the reality of the world; nor is it the reality of standards and values. It is the reality of God as He reveals Himself in Jesus Christ. It is fair to begin by demanding assent to this proposition of anyone who wishes to concern himself with the problem of a Christian ethic.[11]

We must not pass too quickly over the negations in this statement. (In theology, what is negated—as we noted, in passing, about the Barmen Declaration—is often more important than what is affirmed, and affirmations unaccompanied by negations, implicit or explicit, are frequently innocuous.) It is *not*, Bonhoeffer insists, one's own reality; it is *not* the world's reality; and it is also *not* the reality of (one of our favorite and wholly unexamined words today) "values" that constitute the point of vantage, vision, and concern from which Christians develop their ethical responses. In these three negations, Bonhoeffer challenges the very bases on which, I would say, most Christians in North America today *do* in fact proceed ethically: *the self,* with its consciousness and its rights; the *worldview* adopted by one's class, race, gender, interest group, political party, and so forth; and the *moral standards and values* that individuals and groups hope to inculcate. Of course it makes a difference whether these points of departure add up to a morality that is conservative, liberal, or radical. But the point that Bonhoeffer is making (and I find it confirmed almost universally in Christian ethical discourse and behavior on this continent) is that if there is no *other* basis for Christian personal and social ethics than these; if there is no ongoing, grace-given internal critique of these "natural" sources of our moral identity as persons and groups from the side of a distinctively Christian perspective, then Christianity will *not* in fact *engage* its society; it will only *reflect* it.

And precisely that, I think, is what we are doing. Some of us reflect the conservative elements in our society, some the liberal, some the radical. But when is the last time that you read with care a denominational pronouncement on such persistent contemporary ethical questions as the environment or human sexuality, for example, and were able to tell yourself in all honesty that the document in question not only reflected a viable Christian point of view but that it *arrived at this point of view* on this particular subject in a way that was profoundly and not just superficially *theological?* It is not enough for such statements to quote scripture, or to refer to historic creeds, or to use God talk. It is entirely possible (is it not also usual?) to express the most predictable moral inclinations of conservative, liberal, or radical social strata in stained-glass accents, and so to bless with the imprimatur of religion some dimension of the status quo.

When the young Bonhoeffer accused American religion of lacking theological "criticism" and so of having difficulty getting "beyond ethics," he was insisting that the "reality" signified by the name Jesus Christ functions *critically* vis-à-vis the moral assumptions of cultures and their official cults. The Christian evangel opens faith to a new "reality"; ethical thought and deed (which for him are inseparable) involves the disciple community in a continuing struggle to understand and implement (his word for both is "realize") this new reality in the concrete and ever-changing life of the world:

> The problem of Christian ethics is the realization among God's creatures of the revelational reality of God in Christ, just as the problem of dogmatics is the truth of the revelational reality of God in Christ. The place which in all other ethics is occupied by the antithesis of "should be" and "is," idea and accomplishment, motive and performance, is occupied in Christian ethics by the relation of reality and realization, past and present, history and event (faith), or, to replace the equivocal concept with the unambiguous name, the relation of Jesus Christ and the Holy Spirit.[12]

There could hardly be a stronger statement of the theological — indeed, of the trinitarian theological — foundations of Christian ethics. In fact, while Bonhoeffer's *The Cost of Discipleship* could seem to the twenty-year-old that I used to be an almost dangerous, ante-Protestant return to "salvation by works," the effect of his writing as a whole, especially when it is read from the perspective of a North American church that at the same time overemphasized and truncated the ethical dimension of the faith, is to reaffirm the Reformation's foundation of law in the heart of gospel. His book *Ethics* is in a real sense a polemic against the reduction of faith to ethics, and a clarion call to the remnants of Protestantism to distinguish itself from the official morality of their social settings through a lively recall of the "reality" that *God* is bringing to pass in the world through the resurrection and reign of the crucified one. "Christian ethics," he writes, "claims to discuss *the origin* of the whole problem of ethics, and thus professes to be a critique of all ethics simply as ethics."[13]

It is this theological critique of "ethics simply as ethics" and Bonhoeffer's corresponding attempt to establish the ethical thrust of the gospel *itself,* not as an addendum but as part of the grace by which faith if grasped—it is this, I think, that is missed if one goes to Bonhoeffer's last fragments without having traveled along the lonely path that led him to such conclusions. Taken by themselves, and read too hurriedly, the fragments can suggest to the mind already prone to one-dimensional secular activism that what Christianity from now on must mean is a vigilant world-responsibility, enacting Jesus' kind of concern for "others" even though it cannot today assume the transcendent sources of Jesus' concern. Such a credo should not be despised in a world of growing individualism, ethnocentrism, and global violence. But it does not transcend the merely ethical; its imperative, however honorable, lacks an indicative; and it is certainly not what Bonhoeffer struggled for.

Bonhoeffer's ethic, as the key word in my title suggests, was an ethic of Christ's *discipleship*. Discipleship is the constant that runs throughout all of his works. We can be grateful that he was instrumental in reintroducing this word into the Protestant theological vocabulary, for in mainline Protestantism, perhaps beginning with the chief Reformers themselves, it was never a very operative term.

Today I am glad that my first exposure to Bonhoeffer was his *Nachfolge (The Cost of Discipleship)*. If we want to consider movement and *change* in Bonhoeffer's developing thought (and of course he changed; only hardened ideologues do not), the change that matters is not a change in discipleship, with all the christological background thereof, but a change in Bonhoeffer's focus on the *field* and *character* of Christ's discipleship. He never discarded the trinitarian theological foundations of his ethic; he did, however, become aware, the more he was sucked into the vortex of the Nazi *Götterdämmerung,* that "following after" (*nachfolgen*) Jesus Christ in a world-destroying world means becoming in a truly biblical, incarnational sense worldly.

Bonhoeffer himself on one occasion reconsidered this book, his first, and he noted that while he still stood by what he wrote in it, he could see now the dangers of its too-pious adherence to a Christ who transcended time and place. "I discovered later, and I'm still discovering right up to this moment," he wrote in a letter of July 21, 1944,[14] "that it is only by living completely in this world that one learns to have faith. . . . By this-worldliness I mean living unreservedly in life's duties, problems, successes and failures, experiences and perplexities. In so doing we throw ourselves completely into the arms of God, taking seriously, not our own sufferings, but those of God in the world—watching with Christ in Gethsemane. That, I think, is faith; that is *metanoia*; and that is how one becomes a man and a Christian."

It is this *worldly discipleship* of Jesus Christ that constitutes the final, mature statement of the thirty-nine-year-old martyr about the meaning of what Luther named *theologia crucis*. To be a disciple of the crucified one, to receive from the Spirit of the risen Christ the courage of *Jesus'* kind of suffering love, is not to walk away from this world in search of a better, but precisely the opposite— to proceed more and more steadfastly into the very heart of the *civitas terrena,* like the fleeing Peter redirected to burning Rome by the One he met on the Appian Way. Worldly discipleship: These words of Bonhoeffer must not be forgotten; this discipleship can never be sufficiently learned; this legacy remains largely unclaimed by our floundering churches.

5   Emil Brunner
Truth as Meeting

There are persons whose eminence is forever obscured by their proximity to others who, often for reasons quite unrelated to personal merit, are more brightly highlighted by the spotlight of history than they. Emil Brunner is such a person. If I may be forgiven a mixed metaphor, I have always thought of Brunner as having lived his life in the shadow of the Matterhorn—and I mean, of course, in the shadow of his luminous Swiss contemporary, Karl Barth. Even today, more than three decades after his death, Brunner's name is invariably linked with Barth's, and almost always in second position, if not as an afterthought.

Or is Brunner's name heard at all today? As I. John Hesselink suggested in a 1989 essay observing the centennial of Brunner's birth (December 23, 1889), many among today's students of theology scarcely recognize this name, or have read little or nothing of its bearer's voluminous output, more than four hundred separate works.[1] One may even ask whether Brunner can legitimately be considered one of our "remembred voices." Among those who do know a little of him, it is more than likely that the little they know will have filtered down to them through the Barth legend. (Wasn't he the one against whom the mighty Barth hurled his famous "*Nein!*"?) Few North American theological students and clergy under fifty, I suspect, will know that this particular "voice" was the one that first made the "new theology" being spawned in Europe *personally* known to the English-speaking world—partly because, unlike Barth, he understood and spoke English and from his youth onward had much contact with the English-speaking peoples.[2]

Such a fate, insofar as it is a fair reading of the situation, is both undeserved and unfortunate—unfortunate, namely, for *us*. Not only was Brunner a great theologian in his own right, but in *some* ways he speaks more directly to today's ecclesiastical and theological realities than does Barth. As is usually the case with history's favorites, Barth came to the fore for many reasons besides his own unquestionable prowess as a theologian. His clear-cut opposition to Nazism; his association with Barmen and the Confessing Church; his position, at a crucial moment, in a *German* university (Bonn); the sheer vastness of his opus; and (not least of all) the uncompromising character of his kerygmatic theology: all this, and much else, contributed to his prominence. After one has read some of Barth's writings, especially the earlier writings, Brunner's work can seem to lack excitement. Like that of H. R. Niebuhr, it can appear altogether too balanced.[3]

In many respects, however, Emil Brunner was not only Barth's equal but his most challenging critic, for his is the criticism of the friend and ally, the comrade at arms. He shares with Barth the formative foundation of a *biblical* theology deeply informed by the Reformation—though in Brunner's case it was Luther and not Calvin, Barth's more prominent historical mentor, who shaped his attitude toward Holy Scripture.

What Brunner's work accentuates in a way that Karl Barth's does not is what today we should call the *relational* character of all genuinely Christian thought and life. But it is misleading to say that that is what we would call it "today," because Brunner was using that language more than half a century ago. Indeed, nothing is more indicative of the short-lived nature of historical memory than is the current assumption in many quarters that relationality in theology was invented by the present cohort of Christian thinkers. As I shall try to show here, it is the soul of Brunner's entire witness, and he learned it from sources much more ancient than our passing epoch.

This became explicit in 1938 with the publication of lectures given by Brunner a year earlier at the University of Uppsala, Sweden, under the German title *Wahrheit als Begegnung*. This work, from which I have taken the title of the present chapter and which will provide the chief primary source material of my discussion, was not translated into English until 1944, the Second World War having of course disrupted this as it did many other large and small undertakings of ordinary life. The translation by Amandus W. Loos seems excellent, but the title chosen by the publisher was unfortunate: *The Divine-Human Encounter*.[4] While it captures something of the rudimentary emphasis of the book on relationship, this title does not do justice to Brunner's basic thesis that *truth* (*Wahrheit*), in the Judeo-Christian sense, is conceivable only in relational terms—as "meeting" (*Begegnung*).[5] It was partly for this reason that, when this work was republished in revised form in 1964, its new title was *Truth as Encounter*.[6] By this time the language of "encounter" was of course part of the theological vocabulary; I still prefer, however, the earthier and less technical word "meeting," which also better translates the German *Begegnung*.[7]

Brunner himself regarded this comparatively small book as his "most important contribution to the theological concept of knowledge."[8] Indeed, he confessed that he differentiated his own *Dogmatics* from Karl Barth's, not only by the "far more modest proportions" of his work but "above all by the fact that the Christian conception of truth, truth as encounter, revelation conceived as God's self-communication, dominates and permeates the treatment of every single theological topic."[9]

Truth as Encounter represents and documents Brunner's appropriation of the Lutheran-Kierkegaardian approach to Christianity, as it came to him through the fresh interpretations of Ferdinand Ebner and Martin Buber. One must agree with Hesselink when he writes that the "theology of encounter" Brunner outlines in this 1937 treatise, "more than any other aspect of his thought, makes his theology distinctive."[10] Unlike Karl Barth, who rather disdainfully abandoned what he called the "existentialist screaming"[11] that had informed his earlier work, Brunner's theology is profoundly shaped by this school. In his "Intellectual Autobiography," he acknowledges that "in the sphere of philosophy" it was "above all" the work of Ebner and

Buber that stimulated the relational assumption that came to inform his whole position: "Here I saw the rationalistic thought-scheme of object and subject overcome by understanding the human person as basically related to the divine Thou and by the distinction between the I-Thou world and the I-it world."[12] Without qualifying the impact of these thinkers upon his own development,[13] he goes on immediately to trace the antecedents of *their* position to Kierkegaard:

> Neither Ferdinand Ebner nor Martin Buber made a secret of the fact that they owed this most important insight to the Bible and the Christian philosopher, Søren Kierkegaard. Today I, in contrast to Karl Barth, still profess allegiance to this great Christian thinker to whom present-day theology, Catholic no less than Protestant, owes more than to anyone since Martin Luther.[14]

Under the influence of this Jewish and Christian revitalization of biblical theology, Brunner produced in 1935 a work of Christian anthropology, *Der Mensch im Widerspruch* (Eng. trans. *Man in Revolt*, 1947)—a book suppressed by the Nazis and one which, at least in Brunner's own opinion, if taken seriously would have rendered "almost meaningless" Barth's disagreement with him over the qustion of a point of contact (*Anknüpfungspunkt*) between fallen humanity and God. It was in *Wahrheit als Begegnung,* however, that he articulated the central epistemological and hermeneutical understanding that came to inform not only his anthropology but every aspect of Christian teaching. As we turn to reflect on the argument of that book,[15] please take particular notice of two factors: (1) the manner in which Brunner combines the methodological insight concerning the relationality of theological truth with a concern to preserve the essential content of the faith, and (2) the immediate pertinence for our own context of his critique of both objectivistic and subjectivistic approaches to Christianity.

———

In the fine old tradition of establishing one's position by first describing that over and against which it has been forged, Brunner explicates what he means by truth as "meeting" by demonstrating the inadequacies and dangers of the two mutually competitive yet mutually reactive ways in which truth has been conceived throughout most of the history of Christendom.

The first of these—and, as we shall see, the "tendency" of which the European Brunner is most conscious—he terms "Objectivism."

> By Objectivism I understand . . . a tendency of man's spirit and will to get something into his power—to manipulate it like an object in definite ways and within definite limits—something which by its very nature is not under human control.[16]

While this tendency has been blatant in (pre–Vatican II) Roman Catholicism, where "The authority of the divine Word was seized (so to speak) and made available in an ecclesiastical system of authority,"[17] it is amply present as well in Protestantism, as we shall point out. "Always and everywhere the same tendency to seek security rises out of man's sinful, anxious nature and therefore expresses itself wherever men have the Church."[18]

But objectivism "has its counterpart" and rival in subjectivism, which stems from a disposition in the human spirit "at least as elemental [as] and possibly even more primitive" than the quest for security, namely "the urge for freedom and spontaneity." The "egoistic desire for freedom" is challenged by the gospel, with its "obedience-commanding message of the dominion of God"; hence it is not surprising to find subjectivism in the church, for it is part and parcel of the sin that grace makes more visible. While the objectivists "cling to the historical givenness of the revelation," Christian subjectivizers emphasize "the free rule of the Spirit":

> These individualistic enthusiasts have no other criterion or basis for faith than experiencing the impartation of the Spirit. All that is given and established, all fixed doctrine, all ordered office, all ecclesiastical constitution or arrangement—yes, even the fixing of God's Word in the Biblical canon—for them this is at once falsification, torpidity.[19]

"Objectivism is a reaction to Subjectivism"—and vice versa. "In fact, the changing relations between Objectivism and Subjectivism

make up a large part of early, medieval, and modern Church history."[20]

The Reformation, Brunner contends, was at its core a transcendence of this "fatal antithesis." Luther in particular overcame
these opposing tendencies through an epistemological principle
dialectical in nature: "[T]hat is, its form of expression was never
the use of one concept, but always two logically contradictory
ones: the Word of God in the Bible and the witness of the Holy
Spirit, but these understood and experienced, not as a duality, but
as a unity."

> What is of concern [to the Reformers] is the truth given once for
> all, the truth of salvation and revelation clearly discoverable and
> available in the words of the Bible. But this Biblical truth can
> never be considered as available, willy-nilly, at the command of
> the Church in doctrine or dogma, but as the Word of the living,
> present Spirit of God, wherewith the Incarnate Word, Jesus
> Christ Himself, takes possession of our hearts and Himself
> makes His home there.[21]

This "liberating knowledge" at the center of the Reformation did
not, however, endure for long. Already with the close of the Reformation era itself, Protestant orthodoxy represents a new and determined return to objectivism. "The heritage from the Reformation
was not simply lost," but it ceased to inform the mainstream of
Protestantism. (Later, especially in *The Misunderstanding of the
Church,* Brunner will propose that such a dialectic *could* not inform
mainstream Protestantism so long as the latter intended to function
as religious establishment.) In a marvelous image (and Brunner is
very adept at such), he writes: "The age of Orthodoxy appears like
a frozen waterfall—mighty shapes of movement, but no movement." The Bible, conceived of as a book of "revealed doctrine,"
functions as a "paper pope," and theology increasingly devolves
into *"Theologismus"*—theologism: "the urge for an ever-nicer pre-
cision in the formulation of conceptions."[22]

Against this intellectualistic reductionism, a "pietistic reaction"—in short yet another subjectivistic revolt—was inevitable;

and Brunner, who for a time, later on, fell under the influence of the Oxford Group Movement, indicates an obvious sympathy for this reaction. Pietism could legitimately appeal to aspects of Luther, especially over against the "frozen waterfall" of Protestant scholasticism. But subjectivism ultimately led to the "dissolution of theology." With the nineteenth century there was a virtual loss of any objective dimension in the liberal cutting edge of Christianity—a loss especially notorious, Brunner avers, in North America:

> It was reserved for the American "theology" in several of its schools of psychology of religion . . . to carry this tendency to a sort of ultimate extreme, so that in the Chicago school, for example, not much more was left of "religion" than a certain social feeling or value experience, for the truth content of which it was wholly meaningless to ask.[23]

Again, however, predictably enough, the pendulum began to swing back to the other extreme. The corrective was first known as "dialectical theology": "The theme of 'religion' disappeared. People were allowed and wanted to hear again about the saving revelation of the Bible, of Jesus Christ, of the divine covenant of grace. . . . The Church as recipient and proclaimer of the Word of God was again taken seriously."[24] But, though he was himself one of the prime movers of this school, Brunner is already (before 1936!) fully conscious of its pitfalls: "[W]hen the Church is taken seriously, its shadow also immediately appears again: Objectivism. . . . when the Church as a whole must defend itself against a menacing power which threatens its very existence, the temptation becomes strong to imprison the Word of God in a system of human assurances." Thus:

> Quite unnoticed, a *neo-orthodox theology* shapes itself out of the earlier dialectic, and it carries all the characteristic marks of Objectivism: one-sided emphasis on doctrine, identification of doctrine with the Word of God, overvaluation of the formulated creed, of dogma; one-sided prominence given to the objective factor in preaching, in the understanding of the Church, especially from the point of view of doctrine, Sacrament, and office—and not to the fellowship of believers; the Church

considered as institution; neglect of love in favor of Orthodoxy, of practical discipleship in favor of a strict churchly attitude; misunderstanding of the missionary and pastoral task of the Church as a result of a one-sided estimation of the sermon as the didactic expounding of the Bible, and so forth.[25]

Though he immediately qualifies this strong denunciation of "neo-orthodoxy" (read: of the *Barthian* clique!), admitting that it is more accurately described as being "*in the process* of becoming of considerable importance," he cautions that "theological movements, once started, follow their own law and produce specific effects of their own even when quite separated from the original controversial situation."[26]

Especially in view of what we have already observed about "balance" in Brunner's work, it might be supposed that at this point, having illustrated from history the problems he wishes to avoid, he would offer a *via media* that would retain the good implicit in both problematic conceptions of truth while warding off their dangers.[27] For Brunner *does* recognize that both objectivism and subjectivism stem from important and even necessary *intentions* on the part of their proponents. Objectivism is generated by the Christian recognition of the priority and givenness of divine grace, subjectivism by the equally necessary recognition that grace must be received by faith.[28] The problem in both cases is that they serve fundamentally questionable tendencies of the human spirit (for security; for autonomy) and are inevitably driven to excess: "As Objectivism leads to torpidity, so Subjectivism to dissolution." Subjectivism is finally the more dangerous of the two, Brunner insists (though, as we shall see, he is far more concerned with objectivism in this book); for while "What is torpid can be awakened again in life," what is dissolved is no longer in existence."[29] Given the good intentions of each, however, could one not combine the two in ways more favorable to truth orientation than Christian history demonstrates?

Brunner issues a strict denial of such a possibility—and in the process makes his chief point: "There is no right middle way between Objectivism and Subjectivism; there is no correct mean between two errors." The problem, in the first place, is not that the church moves between these two pitfalls, but that both approaches, in framing the quest for truth in the way that they have done, have misrepresented and obscured the nature of truth as it is *biblically* conceived. "The Bible is as little concerned with objective as with subjective truth." With this he returns once more to the *thesis* of the entire exercise, which he states as follows:

[T]he use of the Object-Subject antithesis in understanding the truth of faith . . . is a disastrous misunderstanding which affects the entire content of Christian doctrine. . . . The Biblical understanding of truth cannot be grasped through the Object-Subject antithesis; on the contrary it is falsified through it. . . . where the heart of faith is concerned, . . . the Objective-Subjective correlation must be replaced by one of an entirely different kind.[30]

It is now his task to describe this "entirely different kind" of "correlation." The key to it is relationship, namely, a *living* relationship between God and the human creature, a relationship that must of course be talked about ("How can we not speak of what we have seen and heard?") but can never be adequately described—and certainly not in doctrine!

The Biblical revelation in the Old and New Testaments deals with the relation of God to men and of men to God. It contains no doctrine of God as He is in Himself [*Gott-an-sich*], none of man as he is in himself [*Menschen-an-sich*]. It always speaks of God as the God who approaches man [*Gott-zum-Menschen-hin*] and of man as the man who comes from God [*Menschen-von-Gott-her*]. . . .
. . . [I]n the Bible this two-sided relation between God and man is not developed as doctrine, but rather is set forth *as happening in a story*. The relation between God and man and between man and God is not of such a kind that doctrine can adequately express it in abstract formulas, as it is possible to express abstractly, for instance, the relation between the radius

and the circumference of a circle or the relation between the Beautiful and the Good. It is not a timeless or static relation, arising from the world of ideas—and only for such is doctrine an adequate form: rather the relation is an event, and hence narration is the proper form to describe it. *The decisive word-form in the language of the Bible is not the substantive, as in Greek, but the verb, the word of action. The thought of the Bible is not substantival, neuter and abstract, but verbal, historical and personal. Its concern is not with a relation which exists in and for itself, but with a relation which (so to say) occurs.*[31]

The *truth* that is vouchsafed in this relation can no more be objectivized than it can be subjectivized. What is revealed is not a what but a Who, not an it but a Thou. When the Johannine Jesus declares, "I am the truth" (14:6), he epitomizes the whole biblical attitude toward truth: it cannot be had, possessed, contained, appropriated. It can only be lived, and lived *with*—for it is Person.[32]

> In dealing with genuine, primary faith, i.e., when God reveals Himself to me in His Word, we are not then concerned with a "something." In His Word, God does not deliver to me a course of lectures in dogmatic theology, He does not submit to me or interpret for me the content of a confession of faith, but He makes *Himself* accessible to me. And likewise in faith *I* do not think, but *God leads me to think:* He does not communicate "something" to me, but "Himself."[33]

The only analogy to the "exchange" transpiring in this meeting is "the encounter between human beings, the meeting of person with person"—though this is "*only* an analogy."[34] In meeting other persons, I receive knowledge *about* the other; I may be enriched by that knowledge; "but it never penetrates to the core of my person—it does not transform 'myself.'"[35] Such knowledge "leaves me solitary"—until one of these persons does not merely say 'something' and give 'something' but discloses himself and so gives himself to me."[36] Analogously, knowledge *about* God does not provide the perspective from which theological truth may be contemplated; only knowledge *of* God, which is to say faith, creates such a possibility.

What, in that case, may be said concerning knowledge *about* God—concerning doctrine? Brunner will describe the "positive" relation between faith and doctrine, but he is exceptionally conscious of the recurrent danger of turning faith *into* doctrine; therefore he only approaches the positive explication of this relation as one who is at pains to remind his reader at every turn of that danger. "Faith in doctrine has never yet created new men; on the contrary, whenever it has usurped the place of true faith which is fellowship with God, it has always been singularly lacking in love."[37]

Yet doctrine, with which theology is after all primarily concerned, is not to be dispensed with in favor of a merely spiritualistic intimacy—which would constitute, in fact, a victory of subjectivism. The God who reveals "Himself" and not just "something"—truths, information, data—also *in self-revelation* communicates "something" to us. Apart from this "something," we could make of "God" whatever we wished to make—and we do! To begin with, in the process of God's self-communication "a certain amount of doctrine must be present before living faith can come into being."[38] And revelation, while it is not the revelation *of* doctrine, entails doctrine as the attempt of the disciple community to articulate the truth vouchsafed to it in the revelatory moment, and to distinguish it from falsehood. What is revealed is not doctrine but the Word of God, which transcends all human words, including those of the Bible.

> The relation between doctrine and the Word of God . . . is in the last analysis incommensurable. It must suffice to recognize that an abysmal difference, and yet at the same time a necessary connection, lies between the two. Doctrine alone without the presence of the Holy Spirit is law and betokens Legalism; but human boasting about the freedom of the spirit is egoistic enthusiasm. The Formation insight remains valid: Word of Scripture and Word of Spirit, personal directness in doctrinal indirectness, even as Jesus Christ must fulfil the law in order to free us from it.[39]

Endeavoring throughout, then, to walk this dialectical tightrope between the "abysmal difference" yet "necessary connection" between the divine encountered Word and the human words intended to testify to that ineffable Word (but always tempted to usurp its ultimacy!), Brunner devotes nearly two chapters of his book to what amounts to a mini-dogmatics. What he later undertook in the three volumes of his *Dogmatics,* he attempts here to state succinctly. In every area of doctrine from the Trinity to justification to the church, he indicates how he would attempt to combine his primary accent upon the personal, relational character of theological truth with a rigorous concern for articulating Christian doctrine in a way that is both faithful to the encounter basis of truth (and therefore never smugly satisfied with its expression in dogma) and responsible to the integrity of the biblical story that is the foundation of the Christian apologetic and kerygma. He is at pains throughout to prevent his serious exposition of foundational themes of the faith from devolving into yet another objectivistic articulation of doctrine; at the same time, he is conscious of the danger that the personal, relational framework of the whole will fall into a contentless subjectivism unless the effort is made, in this essentially *methodological* treatise, to demonstrate its concrete application to doctrine. It makes a great deal of difference, he insists throughout, whether one considers any doctrine from the perspective of revealed truths or in the light of the "divine-human meeting" that alone determines what Christians could *mean* by truth.

For instance, on the meaning of *faith,* the "popular conception of faith" from the middle of the second century onward, Brunner declares, has been assent to "truths" (*assensus*), whereas the biblical understanding of faith is *trust* (*fiducia*)—namely trust in God elicited by the experience of God's presence in Jesus Christ, through the divine Spirit.

> This confusion, this replacing of personal understanding of faith by the intellectual, is probably the most fatal occurrence within the entire history of the Church. It has been the cause of the too rapid expansion of Christianity and Ecclesiasticism, which has so heavily encumbered the testimony about the revelation of

salvation in Jesus Christ, and has lessened respect for the Church more than anything else.[40]

A similar approach is made to the Trinity, Christology, the authority of scripture, and the doctrine of sin, of the *imago Dei,* of the church, and so on. In all areas of doctrine, Brunner insists, the neglect and sheer *absence* of the primary relatedness that is the presupposition and foundation of them all, biblically understood, ends in a truly abysmal distortion of each aspect of doctrine. The Thou-I/I-Thou foundation stone of biblical truth is lost, and truth becomes an "it" manipulable by its presumed possessors.

> The truth of which the Bible speaks is always a happening, and indeed the happening of the meeting between God and man, an act of God which must be received by an act of man. The truth acting—this is the characteristic unphilosophical, non-Greek way in which the Bible speaks of truth. In the measure that this understanding of truth becomes alive in it, the Church will itself be renewed again into the true Church. For this renascence we are hoping.[41]

As, after decades of reading only passages of Brunner here and there, I occupied myself with a major rereading of his important works in connection with this chapter, I often found myself becoming rather listless—and sometimes even annoyed. It is at least unfortunate that he so often felt the need to justify and commend his own work—insisting, for instance, that this or that insight, this or that treatise, had been put forward by him long before Barth or Niebuhr or Tillich had thought of it. This is unworthy of the man.

And then there are the passages (for example in the popular little book *Our Faith,* translated into dozens of languages) that can only embarrass thoughtful Christians today, on account of their blatantly exclusivistic Christian claims, their dismissal of other religions, their naive unawareness of the pluralistic character of our global village. Perhaps Brunner is the most chauvinistic Christian-European among these "remembered voices," despite the fact that he had more personal contact with the non-European world than many others, including Barth. His "Intellectual Autobiography" certainly betrays a monolithically Swiss sense of personal identity, with little awareness of the price that that protected and self-protective little nation has paid—and has charged others—for its peace.

When I began to read *The Divine-Human Encounter,* however, I forgot the little dissatisfactions I had felt on the way to it, and by the end of the exercise I had come to the conclusion that, were I teaching systematic theology again full-time today I might well require this book at the beginning of the course. There are two reasons for such a determination, and they relate to the two factors for which, earlier, I asked the reader to be on the alert: Brunner's manner of combining his methodological insight with a concern for theological wholeness, and his exposition of the two primary sources of misunderstanding over against which the character of theological truth ought to be enucleated.

Let me begin with the latter: The propensity of the Christian religion to arrange itself around objectivistic and subjectivistic conceptions of truth is at least as conspicuous in our present context as it was in Brunner's. Indeed, the extremities that are logically begotten by these two historically predictable preferences, together with the inevitable polarization inherent in them, are displayed in present-day North American Christianity more openly than, perhaps, ever before.

On the one hand, a powerful—if not the most powerful, certainly the most vociferous—Christian grouping on this continent today pursues an objectivism of truth more blatant, one-sided, and unnuanced than anything recognizable as Protestant orthodoxy in the seventeenth and eighteenth centuries. Biblicism objectifies truth by declaring it to be found quite literally in the Bible; fundamentalism, with which biblicism may or may not be mingled, identifies truth with supposedly foundational dogmas, acceptance of which is necessary to salvation; religious moralism reduces Christian obedience to conservative moral preferences almost entirely lacking in both sophistication and compassion. The Christian Right, in whatever admixture of biblicism, doctrinalism, or moralism it exists, at bottom *is* the religious tendency toward objectivization taken to its ultimate extent—not to say reduced to absurdity. And surely Brunner is quite right when he locates the *impetus* for this tendency in the human, all-too-human drive for *securitas—and for power*. Ironically, its very potency lies in its simplism: "You want the truth? Well, here it is."

On the other hand, and partly (as Brunner claims) in reaction to this objectivism, we live with a growing "tendency" toward the subjectivization of all religious belief. This too has been carried to extreme lengths undreamt of by Schleiermacher and nineteenth-century liberalism, or even by the "American" religious psychologism alluded to by Brunner in the foregoing. In all the once-mainline churches of this continent, large numbers even of active churchgoers believe in their hearts that what is important religiously is personal experience and feeling, often described now as "spirituality." When this is combined not only with biblical and doctrinal ignorance but with an anti-intellectualism that distrusts and ignores every attempt to achieve theological maturity in the church, it makes for an individualistic subjectivism far beyond anything Brunner had to regret in his European Reformed context.

In addition to that, our situation contains a cultural factor—almost a sea change—that Brunner could not have anticipated, one that greatly enhances the subjectivistic side of this duality. By the end of this most materialistic century, materialism in its various expressions having so visibly demonstrated its incapacity to satisfy the human quest for meaning, *spiritualism* has become a viable alternative even for the most secular. Typically, predictably, this new spirituality in its multitudinous forms appeals to the individualism and privatism that are already deeply rooted in our culture, and further entices its adherents away from the attempt either to think or to act publicly, politically. Moreover, this secular retreat into the interior has profoundly affected liberal and moderate forms of Christianity, thus further tempting church adherents to accentuate the emotive and personal and to ignore the cognitive and public dimensions of their tradition.

Brunner was surely right when he located the psychic impetus for subjectivism in the drive for autonomy over against the heteronomy of authoritarian systems. He was even more prophetic, however, when he declared that subjectivism moves inevitably toward the "dissolution" of theology and the church. In theory, he understood that subjectivism is the greater danger of the two "tendencies," but because he was a European, the product of a society almost over-indoctrinated in the Reformed tradition, he feared objectivism, in practice, more than subjectivism, as this little book amply testifies. Had he been a North American theologian at the end of the century, he would certainly have spent more time in *Wahrheit als Begegnung* warning of the dangers of truth's subjectivization.

The relevance of this work for our context is even more decisive, however, when one recognizes not only that these two "tendencies" are well-represented among us but that, so far as the vast majority of people in and around the churches are concerned, *they represent the only two alternatives:* Either one falls in with the objectifiers (biblicists, fundamentalists, moralists) or one casts one's lot with the subjectifiers (personal piety, the quest for values, etc.). It is rare among us even to discover Christian groupings that find a *via media,* though the attempt is sometimes made. What is almost entirely missing in our Christianity is any commanding sense that truth, according to this tradition, is to be equated with neither the objectification nor the subjectification of faith claims, but requires an entirely different basis and articulation. In short, Brunner's insistence that theological truth is founded upon and inseparable from the "meeting" of Creator and creature has still to be understood and appropriated by us.

And here we are necessarily brought back to the first observation, above: Brunner's attempt to apply this foundational methodological insight to the exposition of what Christians profess. Whether he himself succeeded in doing this is a matter for discussion, but that he pointed the way is in my opinion beyond debate. Perhaps such an attempt must always fail—or at least never wholly succeed. For if one really believes that the God with whom faith has to do is a Thou who defies every reduction to It—as Brunner says, to "something"—then searchers after the *vere theologia* will always have to live with the impossibility of their task.

But that does not mean that the community of faith can afford to resign from the theological thrust implicit in faith. To do so— as for all practical purposes thousands upon thousands of nominal Christians have done—is to pursue fragmentation and dissolution undeterred. The danger of objectification in doctrinalism, biblicism, and moralism is ever present. In some quarters, if not others, even the most lively exposition of the faith will be picked up and hardened into dogma or ideology. Even bread will become stone! And the stone will be thrown at someone! But Brunner's *attempt* is all the same the right one.

It is, in a word, the attempt to contemplate all the many facets of what is entailed in trusting *this* God in the light of the meeting with this God that faith at bottom *means*. If the encounter with the eternal Thou is the very foundation of my and our life, then no aspect of our being and of all being can be understood or discussed apart from this *with*-being. As soon as any element of what Christians profess and proclaim is lifted out of that relational context and made interesting in itself, it is a candidate for the exact distortions that Brunner depicts. Not only the great areas of doctrine (theology, Christology, anthropology, ecclesiology, eschatology) but *all doctrine* (creaturehood, sin, *imago Dei,* worship and sacraments, ethics, etc.) must be contemplated and articulated under the rubric of the Emmanuel principle—which is no principle, but a reality and *the* reality without which the whole enterprise of theology is "sounding brass and clanging cymbal."

H. Richard Niebuhr
Christ and (Post-Christian) Culture

Many Christian professionals, if asked to identify H. Richard
Niebuhr's most important contribution to Christian theology in the
twentieth century, would turn immediately to the two best known
of his eight published books. *The Meaning of Revelation* and
Christ and Culture. The first, which is often regarded as Niebuhr's
finest work, is a terse and persuasive exposition of the *kind* of understanding of revelation that we have already discussed in connection with the work of Emil Brunner. *Christ and Culture,*
written some ten years later and dedicated to "Reinie," his elder
brother, remains a useful and imaginative classification of the
ways Christians have conceived and lived the relation of their faith
to their cultural contexts.

Both books have continuing importance for Christians in North
America and are frequently cited. Yet neither, I think, considered
as response to the principal question it addresses, quite captures either the theological center of Niebuhr's thought or its real significance for us today. Each draws attention to a specific problem:
defining the nature of revelation in a rationalistic, data-obsessed
civilization, and describing the strengths and weaknesses of five
ways in which Christians relate to their host societies. Concentrat-
ing on these problems, which are certainly real enough still, can
nevertheless obscure the faith perspective from which H. Richard
Niebuhr wrote. What is forgotten regularly, even by those who remember this voice, is that Niebuhr developed his theology of revelation and of culture in the ways that he did because he adhered
to certain foundational convictions about the core of Christian belief. Unfortunately, like his elder brother, he did not venture into
an extended exposition of those convictions. There is, however,

enough explicit and implicit evidence in what he did write to give us a very strong testimony to the belief that informed this provocative Yale theologian.

In this chapter, as in the others, I shall concentrate on one aspect of Niebuhr's theological foundations, but one that for him as for all Christians is by definition central and indispensable: his Christology—or rather, to speak more accurately, the place of Christology in his theocentric faith. I have chosen this subject for two reasons: first, because it is abundantly clear that Niebuhr himself understood Christology to be both the greatest opportunity and the greatest problem of the Christian movement in the contemporary world; second, because I believe that nothing is more needful for *us* to hear from this eminent teacher of our immediate past than his manner of contemplating Jesus Christ, for he does so both as a Christian apologist fully conscious of the pluralistic character of our society, and as a churchman living between the extremes of a conservative absolutism that substitutes the divinization of Jesus for incarnation of the Word, and an inchoate liberal theism that begs the question, Why Jesus?

As Christianity emerges from its Constantinian cocoon into the large and multiform world of beliefs and unbeliefs, there is a conspicuous tendency for Christians unused to reasoned defence of their faith to seek refuge from challenges to it by adopting doctrinaire expressions of belief. Declaration is substituted for *apologia* or genuine confession of faith. Especially in the North American context, such expressions characteristically include the elevation of the Bible to a status of infallibility and the reduction of revelational truth to dogmatic propositions. Most importantly, however, they focus on Jesus Christ, and particularly upon that aspect of the doctrine technically referred to as Christology, as distinct from soteriology. Here, the key term is Christ's "divinity," which is allegedly proved by his miraculous birth, his miracles, and his bodily resurrection.

That such code language (for that is what it is) should be prominent among fundamentalists carries with it no surprise; in North America that phenomenon has been with us for more than a hundred years. But that declarations of this nature should have come to dominate discussions within the so-called mainstream Protestant churches in North America is, after all, quite astonishing. When the only alternative to a vague theological liberalism within that constituency appears to be resort to an orthodoxy highly colored by fundamentalist rhetoric, one can only conclude that the powerful testimony of the theologians we are grouping here under the nomenclature "neo-orthodoxy" has been lost on the churches. If what these theologians have taught is, in significant ways, forgotten even among the professionals who remember their voices, it often seems that their impact has not been felt at all among the churches!

Whether this represents a failure of seminaries to teach, or of the teaching elders (i.e., the clergy) to teach what they have been taught, or whether it constitutes a failure more profound such as the general trivialization and sentimentalization of all religion in the age of media is a matter for discussion. What is obvious is that the ecclesiastical debates of the times, whether in matters doctrinal or moral, evince little if any influence from the side of the great and creative theological ferment that occurred during the first part of this century.

As I write, for instance, a controversy rages within my own denomination, the most liberal church of my country and certainly one of the most liberal of the continent. Individuals and collectivities from whom one would not anticipate such behavior range themselves against a significant portion of the denomination's leadership, and join the chorus of those who cry that the line must be held. And for most the line is held by waving slogans rendered devoid of either theological or human meaning by their overuse within certain segments of Christendom: "the divinity of Christ," "the resurrection," "Bible truth," and so on. (I shall return to this in my Conclusions.)

It appears that Christology constitutes a highly problematic area of doctrine, and precisely at a time when it ought to provide the Christian movement with its most distinctive—and potentially most relevant—witness. If Christianity is to survive the demise of Christendom, and to survive *as Christianity,* it will have to discover again, as it has sometimes done in the past, how to see and present Jesus Christ as the focal point of its *apologia*—and *not,* therefore, as an arbitrary item in the church's line of self-defence! Paul rightly insists that the gospel of "Jesus Christ and him crucified" is a point of stumbling and offence. But it is that *only* if and when it is able to make its way through all the bric-a-brac of worldly rationalization and self-deceit to confront human beings in the reality of their historical existence. The foolishness of the gospel should not be confused with worldly rejection of mere religious dogmatism. Slogans like "the divinity of Christ" do not achieve anything remotely resembling the *skandalon* of the cross; they can be—and regularly are—heard with perfect indifference.

What is remarkable about the thought of H. R. Niebuhr is that it combines a constructive recognition of the centrality and indispensability of Jesus as the Christ with a critical awareness of the temptation of Christians to misuse precisely this center—and through their misuse, to jettison and destroy it. Christians yield to that temptation when they substitute for a fully *trinitarian* understanding of God what Niebuhr called "unitarianism of the second person of the Trinity." When Jesus Christ becomes (to paraphrase the language of J. A. T. Robinson) "all the God of God there is"; when the whole substance of the faith is subsumed under the confession of his redemptive sovereignty; when what people are asked to believe is that "Jesus is God," the *skandalon* of faith is reduced to ordinary absurdity and offensiveness—*particularly* in a pluralistic society. Such Christomonism has always been suspect. Those who embraced it in the early church, including the Monophysites whom Chalcedon itself rejected, were declared heretical. But in a society like ours, where sensitive Christians themselves have become conscious of the unwarranted exclusivity of so many of our conventional claims, it is necessary for all Christians to become informed and nuanced in their witness to Jesus as the Christ. Testimony to the Christ must be set within a theological framework that *transcends without superseding* Jesus of Nazareth. That is what the *logos* imagery did for early Christians in *their* pluralistic context, and it is what responsible Christian apologetics has always had to attempt.

H. Richard Niebuhr, in this respect very representative of the Reformed tradition as exemplified by Jonathan Edwards,[1] intended his entire theological and ethical testimony to be *theocentric*. For Christology this theocentrism means: Jesus Christ is the revealer *of God*. In other words, the function of Christ's centrality for Christians is that he points beyond himself to an Ultimacy that he reflects and even may be said to embody, but does not wholly contain or exhaust. In drawing faith's attention to himself, Jesus points simultaneously beyond himself to God, so that our faith would not be what he intends it to be were it to remain transfixed upon him. It is indeed *because* the object, that is, the living Subject, of the faith that Jesus elicits *transcends* Jesus that faith focuses *upon* Jesus, acknowledging him to be the Christ.

Niebuhr did not write extensively about the Trinity, but he clearly intended his theocentrism to be understood within the context of a trinitarian conception of deity. In a 1951 essay entitled "An Attempt at a Theological Analysis of Missionary Motivation," he wrote:

> The theological standpoint from which I shall endeavor to view these [missionary] motives is Trinitarian, that is to say, it is neither Christocentric, nor spiritualistic, nor creativistic, but all of these at once. In this sense it seeks to be theocentric. I seek to understand as one who believes in God, the Father, Almighty Creator of heaven and earth and in Jesus Christ his Son, who for us men and our salvation was incarnate, was crucified, raised from the dead and reigns with the Father as one God, and in the Holy Spirit who proceeds from the Father and the Son (from the Father as much as from the Son), and who is the immanent

divine principle not only in the church but in the world created
and governed by God.[2]

What this statement connotes, seen within the social and religious
context in which it was made, is Niebuhr's wish to correct the mis-
interpretation and misuse of one dimension of trinitarian theology
by accentuating the other dimension of this same doctrine: namely,
that dimension of the Trinity that stresses the unity principle, without which the principle of differentiation or distinction within the
godhead leads to tritheism, or, as Niebuhr felt had happened in modern theology, to concentrate so exclusively upon the Christ as to end
in "a new unitarianism of the second person of the Trinity."[3] Seen
from one perspective, trinitarian theology evolved in the early
church in order to safeguard the uniqueness and ultimacy of the person and work of Jesus Christ, but from another perspective it origi-
nated with the need of the developing church in *its* pluralistic context
to set its testimony to Jesus Christ within the framework of a larger
mystery still, the mystery of the transcendent and immanent Source
of all life. The perspective that one brings to this "gospel *in nuce*,"
as the Trinity has been called, is determined in large measure by
one's perception of the theological *errors* and *dangers* present in
one's ecclesiastical context. H. Richard Niebuhr perceived—in my
opinion quite rightly—that, on account of its traditional penchant for
simplistic doctrinal conservatism, aggravated in some quarters by
misrepresentation of the very "neo-orthodoxy" we are investigating,
the greatest danger to Protestant Christianity in America was the
danger of an overemphasis upon the unity principle applied in practice to Christology. What had to be stressed, therefore, was the trinitarian intention of placing the Christ within a fully *theo*-logical
framework: Jesus Christ is the revelation *of God*.

Does *Jesus alone* reveal God? One suspects that Niebuhr would
have wanted to press this question further had he lived into the later
part of the twentieth century. The point, however, is that on the basis of this theocentric trinitarianism *he could have done precisely
that*; for clearly a Christ who is our Christian "way" to a God who
transcends without superseding him necessitates the positing of a

God to whom there may well be other ways as well. Thus in one of his most evocative sentences, Niebuhr articulates a direction that ought to be taken very seriously today by all who are attempting to discover how Christians living within an increasingly pluralist and post-Christendom culture may retain the christological basis of their faith without reducing the Christ to a *false* scandal:

> I do not have the evidence which allows me to say that the miracle of faith in God is worked only by Jesus Christ and that it is never given to men outside the sphere of his working, though I may say that where I note its presence I posit the presence also of something like Jesus Christ.[4]

The christological—even christocentric—*basis* of this sentence cannot be missed: Jesus Christ constitutes, for its writer, the one through whom the very character of God, and faith in God, is determined. But neither can the careful reader ignore the assumption of the sentence that, since it is *God* whom Christians believe they glimpse through the mediation of Jesus Christ, they are enabled and obliged to be open to intimations of this same God *wherever they find them*. In Luther's language, the "revealing God" (*Deus revelatus*) being simultaneously the "hidden God" (*Deus absconditus*), there is a mystery, depth, and *breadth* in God's being and acting that is not limited to the *Christian* apprehension of deity.

Is Niebuhr guilty of subordinating the Son to the Father? John Godsey suggests as much when he asks whether Niebuhr has not subsumed the Son and the Spirit under his overarching conception of the transcendent God:

> [T]he question can be asked of Niebuhr whether, with his tremendous emphasis on monotheism, he does justice to the doctrine of God as Trinity. Niebuhr has well depicted the problem of unitarianisms of the first, second, and third 'persons' of the Trinity, but has he himself been able to formulate an understanding of God that escapes the charge of unitarianism? Niebuhr never tired of stressing God's oneness, but is the oneness predicated in abstraction from God's revelation in Christ?[5]

Hans Frei also speaks of Niebuhr's "subordination of Christology to theology" and cites this as Niebuhr's "only qualification of [Jonathan] Edwards."[6] Frei's formulation of the matter, however, provides the best clue to a fair response to the question: to say that "Christology" is subordinated to theology is not to say that *Jesus Christ* is subordinated to God; as person, Jesus is not reducible to Christology or (more accurately) to any of history's many Christologies, which are limited and biased interpretations of the Christ that regularly tell one more about their devisers than they do about the Christ. It is of a piece with the very Reformed conception of theological method that Niebuhr found in Edwards, and himself represents, that the confession of belief in the *sole glory of God* relativizes all else, including theology. Perhaps especially theology! Niebuhr's so-called historicism is a direct consequence of this insistence. Theologians are historically conditioned persons whose attempts to comprehend the eternal are necessarily relative.[7] As much as Reinhold, who frequently railed against all religious "pretentions to finality," H. Richard Niebuhr feared the hubris of theology and its consequences, particularly, for Christology. Thus, responding to the familiar question about revealed and natural knowledge of God, he wrote:

> Confessional theology must approach the problem with the resolution to restrain its desire to prove the superiority of Christianity to other religions or of a Christian theology to philosophy by pointing to the church's possession of revelation. The revelation of God is not a possession but an event, which happens over and over again when we remember the illuminating center of our history. What we can possess is the memory of Jesus Christ, but what happens to us through that memory we cannot possess. What is more important, revelation turns against the self which would defend itself; it is the happening which leaves the men to whom it happens without excuse.[8]

This kind of wise caution where all theology, and especially revealed theology concerning the Christ, is concerned, does not, however, amount to subordinationism of the Son to the Father in the classical, metaphysical sense—which in any case, as we shall see, Niebuhr could not have embraced. Jesus Christ, without becoming the whole object of Christian faith and devotion, remains for Niebuhr the revelatory entrée to the whole. This, as I read it, is the point James Gustafson makes in his response to the aforementioned essay of Francis Schüssler Fiorenza. While historical existence is existence-in-motion, God for Niebuhr is "the centre of gravity," and the "fixed confessional point" with which Christian faith has to do is Jesus Christ. This Niebuhr articulated

> among other places, in *The Responsible Self* (1963). I quote only the nub of it. For Christians Jesus Christ "turns their reasoning around so that they do not begin with the premise of God's indifference but of his affirmation of the creature, so that the *Gestalt* which they bring to their experiences of suffering as well as joy, of death as well as of life, is the *Gestalt,* the symbolic form, of grace" (175–76). As circumspect discussions in the lectures *Faith on Earth* show, this affirmation was not made trivially or easily in the light of much experience.[9]

If Jesus Christ is to "turn human reasoning around," however, it is not enough for the church simply to *affirm* that Jesus is for faith the revealer of God. Declaratory theological language is part and parcel of the mentality of the imperial church; it must give way now to the demand for reasons for the hope that is in us—a demand that belongs as much to faith as to worldly skepticism. Niebuhr rejected metaphysical speculations about Christ's "nature" not only because they were abstract but because they did not advance beyond mere declaration and spurious authoritarianism: "Jesus is *divine,* therefore you had better believe what we say!" In the missionary situation of the contemporary church, as in the preestablished early church, Christian testimony to Jesus as God's revelation requires concrete description of Jesus' historical person as distinct from formulas concerning its alleged composition. To call Jesus "divine and human" in accordance with Chalcedon, or to take refuge in the once-accessible apologetic device of the Logos, or to indulge in monotonously generous use of the titles "Lord" and "Savior" and even

"Christ," is actually to give little if any real content to this name. Even in its own time, to say nothing of today, all such language was dependent upon a far more explicit and down-to-earth picture of the one concerning whom it was made. *Jesus preceded Christology,* and must always do so if what is truly *essential* about him as incarnation of the very mind and heart of God is to be sustained: namely, that he is *person,* Thou. Today, when all the titles assigned him by the developing church, including "Christ," are part of a linguistic past that is virtually inaccessible to our contemporaries, the Christian confession of Jesus' centrality is obliged to return to the most rudimentary testimony of the Gospels to his life and death. *That,* with all of the limitations thereto pertaining, is nevertheless where evangelical opportunity must be found—and it may be found there, because there are qualities in this narrative that are able still to stir the imagination, move the will, and change the heart.[10]

What is a Christian? A Christian is "one who believes in Jesus Christ," answers H. Richard Niebuhr. But he knows, as we all do, that this says both everything and nothing, and therefore he immediately specifies:

> [A Christian is] one who counts himself as belonging to that community of men for whom Jesus Christ—his life, words, deeds, and destiny—is of supreme importance as the key to the understanding of themselves and their world, the main source of the knowledge of God and man, good and evil, the constant companion of the conscience, and the expected deliverer from evil.[11]

Even this kind of specification does not suffice, however, for "so manifold [is] the interpretation of [Jesus'] essential nature, that the question must arise whether the Christ of Christianity is indeed one Lord." Nevertheless—and here Niebuhr's identity with Reformed theology's *sola scriptura* is evident!—the "fact remains that the Christ who exercises authority over Christians or whom Christians accept as authority is the Jesus Christ of the New Testament," "a person with definite teachings, a definite character, and a definite fate," who "can never be confused with a Socrates, a Plato or an Aristotle, a Gautama, a Confucius, or a Mohammed, or even with an Amos or Isaiah."

To be sure, this point of concentration and departure is not without its inherent problems, two in particular: the first is that it is impossible to articulate by means of concepts and propositions a principle that presents itself in the form of a person; the second is that it is impossible to say anything about this person without importing into one's statements assumptions and biases and concerns of one's own.

In contrast to the many theologies that are frightened off by these difficulties and turn, ironically, to abstract foundations far more questionable, Niebuhr dismisses such faintheartedness in two splendidly bold sentences worthy of a Luther: "If we cannot say anything adequately, we can say some things inadequately. If we cannot point to the heart and essence of this Christ, we can at least point to some of the phenomena in which his essence appears."

The phenomena to which Niebuhr, describing himself as "a moralist," turns are five "virtues" of Jesus Christ derived from the biblical witness to him, as appropriated by various segments of the Christian movement. "By the virtues of Christ we mean the excellences of character which on the one hand he exemplifies in his own life, and which on the other he communicates to his followers." Niebuhr does not consider this the only way of representing the life of Jesus—"the resultant portrait needs to be complemented by other interpretations of the same subject"—but it is a means of responding to the question of Jesus' identity, and of doing so in a manner that leads simultaneously to the question of his redemptive work.

The five "virtues" or "excellences" are: love, hope, obedience, faith, and humility. In each case, Niebuhr identifies the segment of the Christian community that accentuates that particular virtue, and critiques the one-sided concentration upon it by noting its separation from the other virtues and its abstraction from the relationship of Jesus with God. Thus love, upon which Christian liberalism concentrates, becomes sentimentalistic—"the love of love"—when it is treated as an ideal. God defines love, not vice versa: "Though God is love, love is not God for him [Jesus]; though God is one, oneness is not his God." Love is not a goal for which Jesus strives, but his response to the love of God: "It was not love but God that filled his soul."

Similarly, hope, the virtue too exclusively pursued by the eschatologists (Schweitzer being the best-known spokesman), must not be turned into an ideology, a dogma. Jesus does not hope in a theory about history, he hopes in God. "Though the Jesus described in the New Testament was clearly animated by an intense hope, yet it seems evident that the reality present to him as the author of the future was not a course of history, dogmatically conceived."

The third virtue, obedience, has been stressed by Bultmann and other Christian existentialists, but it "has been essentially abstracted from the realization of God which makes all the virtues of Jesus Christ radical." Existentialism gives us "a caricature of the New Testament Christ" by presenting him along the lines of a "twentieth century view of freedom." Jesus was "obedient," as the Gospels and epistles insist, but obedient, not to an abstraction, "an Unconditioned," but to a creating and governing God of love in whom he has faith.

But faith, the fourth virtue, which is the classical Protestant excellence, can also be torn from its context and become a virtue in itself. Jesus' faith is trust in God "despite his skepticism" about human beings. With humility, the virtue stressed by Christian monasticism, something similar must be said: his humility is profound—"There is indeed something disproportionate about the humility of Jesus Christ." But he does not pursue humility as an end in itself; it is, rather, a consequence of knowing himself standing before God—"He neither exhibited nor commended and communicated the humility of inferiority-feeling before other men."

"Thus," Niebuhr concludes, "any one of the virtues of Jesus may be taken as the key to the understanding of his character and teaching; but each is intelligible in its apparent radicalism only as a relation to God," and it is preferable "not to attempt to delineate him by describing one of his excellences but rather to take them all together."

> [I]t seems evident that the strangeness, the heroic stature, the extremism and sublimity of this person, considered morally, is due to that unique devotion to God and to that single-hearted trust in Him which can be symbolized by no other figure of speech so well as the one which calls him Son of God. . . . No one can know the Son without acknowledging the Father.

What Niebuhr is doing in this may seem little more than an application of Schleiermacher's description of Jesus' highly developed God-consciousness, and indeed one may sense Schleiermacher behind the scenes. But Niebuhr has more in mind than refurbishing Schleiermacher's portrait of Jesus as the ultimate God-oriented human being. In his way—that is, within the context of his theocentrism and his relational understanding of the faith—Niebuhr is attempting to salvage from the "two natures" Christology what is of permanent value and can be understood in a postmetaphysical culture. Jesus' humanity—true humanity (*vere homo*)—is expressed in the love, hope, obedience, faith, and humility that turns him toward God; and his "moral sonship" of God in turn directs him unerringly toward humanity and creation. Jesus' life thus "involves the double movement—with men toward God, with God toward men; from the world to the Other, from the Other to the world; from work to Grace, from Grace to work; from time to the Eternal and from the Eternal to the temporal":

> In his moral sonship to God Jesus Christ is not a median figure, half God, half man; he is a single person wholly directed as man toward God and wholly directed in his unity with the Father toward men. He is mediatorial, not median. He is not a centre from which radiate love of God and of men, obedience to God and to Caesar, trust in God and in nature, hope in divine and in human

action. He exists rather as the focusing point in the continuous alternation of movements from God to man and man to God; and these movements are qualitatively as different as are *agape* and *eros,* authority and obedience, promise and hope, humiliation and glorification, faithfulness and trust.[12]

It would be absurd, of course, to propose that the few paragraphs devoted by H. Richard Niebuhr to Christology in *Christ and Culture,* even when they are supplemented by scattered references in his other published and unpublished works, can suffice as a statement of the alternative approach that Christian faith and theology today ought to take to this all-important and foundational question. But I believe that Niebuhr has pointed the way, both to overcoming the sterility of a Christology stuck in the past and mired in slogan and shibboleth, and to exploring a witness to "the second person of the Trinity" that sets the mystery and meaning of Jesus Christ in the context of a love that exceeds *all* its appropriations in doctrine and deed.

Suzanne de Diétrich
The Word of God for the People of God

When in 1950 the Protestant theological faculty at Montpellier, France, conferred on her an honorary doctorate in theology, Dean Henri Leenhardt introduced Suzanne de Diétrich as one whose name had been revered "for almost forty years by generations of young people" and a person "of whom one can say that she is the greatest lay theologian of our time."[1] Whether such a claim can be sustained—indeed, whether any Christian should ever be called "the greatest"—it is beyond dispute that this diminutive French baroness, obliged by a congenital infirmity to walk with two sticks throughout her long life, exercised an immense influence upon generations of European and international students, and upon the course of Christian theology in the twentieth century. Her contribution to ecumenical Christianity is still insufficiently recognized, particularly in North America; in this as in many other ways she is representative of the many scholarly and devoted women who, largely unsung, were influential animators of the theological renewal of the church during the first half of this century. Like so many of these women (one thinks of such names as Charlotte von Kirschbaum[2], Ellen Flessemann-Van Leer, Ursula Niebuhr, Hulda Niebuhr, Olive Wyon, Dorothy Sayers, Suzanne Bidgrain, Kathleen Bliss, Marie-Jeanne de Haller Coleman, Margaret Prang, Anne Bennett, to name only a few), de Diétrich worked closely with male colleagues and friends whose names were more prominent among their contemporaries—in her case, especially Visser 't Hooft, Hendrik Kraemer, Pierre Maury, and others. Indeed, she frequently expressed the view that "true humanity," as well as the most interesting scholarship, "matures best in the complementarity of women and men,"[3] and herself seems to have preferred to work with men.[4] But that predisposition neither detracted from her innately feminist convictions nor diminished the originality and independence of her work.

It is more than symbolic of her spirit that the young Suzanne de Diétrich became "the second woman in French-speaking Europe to complete her engineering studies successfully."[5] That she took up engineering despite her keener interest in the classics and philosophy, was of course a consequence of her destiny as perhaps the only member of her generation who could assume hands-on responsibility in the immense de Diétrich industry of her native Alsace. But that she persevered and, in 1913, graduated in a field entirely dominated by men; and that, having done so, she then, through her conversion and her immersion in the life of the Student Christian Movement, sought her vocation in a completely different sphere, tells one a good deal about her character.

De Diétrich's views on women, which are both implicit and explicit in her writings, seem not to have changed basically from the points that she stressed at Stockholm in 1914 when, at an international Christian conference of the type that was to become familiar to her, she presented a lecture on the civic duties of women. Hans-Ruedi Weber summarizes the lecture as follows:

> She presented two theses: "(1) The emancipation of women is necessary from three points of view: juridical, economic and political. (2) This emancipation, a consequence of the principles expounded by Christ centuries ago, must be realized in the spirit of Christ if it is to become truly liberating." Suzanne substantiated her first thesis with a wealth of information and statistics from all over the world, showing that "feminism is not a passing wave but a great flood tide whose irresistible flow carries the whole of society to as yet unknown new shores." What she said in her second thesis might not have pleased all the feminists: "It is not the fact that women will have the vote that will change the world, but the fact that they take seriously their social responsibility."[6]

It is not, however, for her feminism but for her work as a biblical interpreter and communicator that I have felt it necessary to include her in this study of "remembered voices." To be sure, her voice is remembered by few North Americans, relatively speaking. By comparison with the other figures treated in this study, de Diétrich neither wrote extensively nor achieved widespread recognition. Nevertheless, far from including her here in order to achieve some semblance of gender balance, I do so because she contributed something unique to this movement of Christian renewal—something that she shares, to be sure, with several others among both women and men associated with that movement, but something she represented with a special kind of purity and consistency: namely, the recovery of the *sola scriptura* principle of the Reformation in its most concrete and practical intention. To state the matter in a word: she exemplifies more straightforwardly than any of the others considered in this book what it means that the Bible is the church's foundational charter and guide, and that it is intended *for the people,* the whole *laos,* not only for scholars and professionals. My purpose in this chapter will be, therefore, to elaborate on that theme, illustrating its meaning by reference to de Diétrich's slim volumes (which are mere documentary testimonials to an entire life of active teaching), and drawing from this certain conclusions that I feel are imperative for present-day Christians at a vital point of transition in our history.

It will be instructive to begin by noting how Suzanne de Diétrich herself perceived the character and progress of the so-called neo-orthodox movement. In a 1955 essay for *The Student World* entitled "The Biblical Foundation," she wrote the following summary of what was occurring, as she saw it, in the 1930s:

> A theological revolution swept over Europe which was soon to mark deeply the life of the [World Student Christian] Federation. Barth and Brunner were its early sponsors; the Confessing Church in Germany became a living embodiment of this theological renewal, often called neo-orthodoxy. The word of

God was again proclaimed as a living power, the power by which the church lives. Then the rediscovery of the word led to a rediscovery of the church. Neo-orthodoxy cuts across old categories of fundamentalism and liberalism. The written word is only the medium through which God speaks his living word to us here and now, but it is the necessary medium, chosen by God for this purpose. The whole Bible tells about the redeeming activity of God, and its centre is the incarnation, death and resurrection of Jesus Christ. The parts must be interpreted in the light of the whole, starting from the centre, which is God in Christ.[7]

This thumbnail sketch of the "theological revolution" under discussion contains, in its simplicity and directness, several points that are ordinarily overlooked—even by those who have some familiarity with the so-called giants of this movement. The first and most important point, of course, is that it was a "revolution" inspired *chiefly* by a rediscovery of the Bible. Certainly that rediscovery occurred under auspicious contextual circumstances: the failure of the modern vision, the struggle of the working classes against the excesses of unchecked capitalism, the outbreak, in 1914, of a violent and terrible war, the "death of God" and of human ideals, the capitulation of the religion of progress—all that. All that, however, would never by itself have inspired a renewal of theology and church. We know that for millions of ordinary people and for many brilliant and articulate thinkers, the devastations of the first decades of this century evoked nothing but depression and hopelessness! Many Christians themselves, caught up in the liberal euphoria of the nineteenth century, were reduced to speechlessness and disillusionment by these occurrences. It was only as the more imaginative (or perhaps more desperate!) among Christians were forced to rethink their entire project in dialogue with the scripture that the courage and wisdom were found to stem the tide of secular ennui and nihilism. Too easily we forget that the opening manifestos of "neo-orthodoxy" were neither ecclesiastical pronouncements like Barmen nor theological treatises (not, at any rate, in the usual and unfortunate sense of that term!) but biblical commentaries and exegetical sermons—notably, of course, Karl Barth's *Römerbrief*. It was out of this fresh encounter with "the strange, new world in the Bible" (Barth) that both *theology* and *church* renewal, including the ecumenical movement itself, gradually evolved; and without that biblical inspiration neither theology nor church could have accomplished anything!

A second point made by de Diétrich's summation is almost as important as the first: namely, that the "neo-orthodoxy" resultant upon this fresh encounter with scripture "cuts across old categories of fundamentalism and liberalism." The truth is, prior to the initial scriptural expositions of Barth, Thurneysen, Brunner, and the others, the Bible had been effectively silenced for thinking people by its captivation *by both* fundamentalism and liberalism, as well as their absurd polarization as its dominant interpreters. Fundamentalists reduced the scriptures to an unlikely combination of factual and supernatural data wholly incompatible with both ancient and contemporary understandings of the nature of truth. Liberals reduced the Bible to historical writings, decipherable only to the textually and historically informed, and incapable either of exercising spiritual authority or inspiring awe. If "neo-orthodoxy" cut across this deadlock, it was only because it was able to revive and reinterpret the Reformers' understanding of the Bible, which upholds the positive motivation behind both fundamentalism and liberalism while rejecting their reductionism. Clearly, contra biblicism, a faith that identifies God's living Word (*Logos*) with a *life* cannot be satisfied with mere words, however inspired. But, contra modernism, what besides mere words can bear adequate and nuanced testimony to a life, *that* life included, and to the transcendence to which that life points? It seems reasonable enough—even if it is paradoxical—that while nothing, including Holy Writ, can usurp the centrality and sovereignty of the living God, scripture can and does nevertheless bear testimony to that God in a unique and irreplaceable manner. All the same, it is the tragedy of modern Christianity that this paradox of biblical authority that lies at the heart of the Reformation was never really appropriated by Protestantism, which, in consequence, still today regularly bifurcates into literal-absolutist and historical-relativist forms of reductionism.

Suzanne de Diétrich, like Barth, Brunner, and all the others whom we have treated here, each in his or her own way, understood this paradox (if such it is) very well indeed: "The written word is only the medium through which God speaks his living word to us here and now; but it is the necessary medium." What de Diétrich understood *better* than the others, however, was that *this insight concerning the nature of biblical authority is only as valuable as its implementation in the actual life of the Christian community.* As theory, as theology, it is interesting to those for whom doctrine matters greatly, but unless this manner of regarding the Bible comes to inform the typical self-understanding and behavior of the Christian community, it will make very little difference to the vast majority of churchfolk *or* to the life of the world for which the gospel is intended. Unless they *practice* biblical exposition so understood, churchfolk will inevitably drift into literalistic or relativistic conceptions of truth—as for all intents and purposes they have in fact done throughout this century.

Suzanne de Diétrich is among the relatively few who have made it their business to carry the Bible into the heart of the congregation and beyond, and so to render the Reformation's primary methodological principle, the *sola scriptura,* real and concrete, and not merely another typically Protestant dogma and distinguishing feature. We shall fail to grasp what she was about unless we realize that she conducted her Christian witness *in the midst of the modern university,* that is, at the center of the secular world's bid for truth, *controlling* truth. For thousands of university students she made the Bible a book that *speaks*—or rather, through which God may speak; a book more compelling than Marx's *Das Kapital,* by which so many students of her era were enticed; a book that is *never* exhausted by its most enthusiastic champions, that always transcends its best interpreters, that nevertheless offers itself wholeheartedly and humbly to those who hunger and thirst for understanding.

How, precisely, did de Diétrich go about this labor of interpretation?

—————————————————

Some background comments in response to this question will help to set the tone for more specific observations. It is evident both from her own writings and from the intriguing biographical study by Hans-Ruedi Weber, as well as the testimony of friends who knew her,[8] that de Diétrich was a modern person for whom neither theological dogmatism nor biblical literalism could have had any real appeal. She was not only cultured, widely read, and well educated, as one would expect of a person of her social status and heritage, but beyond that, she was clearly a Reformed Protestant in the classical sense of the term, though without a hint of anti-Catholicism and not given to adulation where John Calvin was concerned![9] That is to say, she brought to reflection on the faith the same kind of critical awareness, practicality, and honest doubt that she applied to all significant experience.

At the same time, at least from the point of her "resolute turning to Christ in 1907–08,"[10] de Diétrich was evidently a genuinely pious person, who considered study and prayer inseparable, and whose life was at least as much a matter of dialogue with God as that of her famous compatriot Simone Weil. She was never "bibliolatrous,"[11] yet she expected of the biblical text more than information and understood her biblical teaching to be a matter of spiritual encounter and genuine evangelism, not merely education. "I never speak to them *about* the gospel," said one of her friends, Charles Grauss, concerning his relationship with his fellow soldiers (he was himself killed in battle in 1918), "but I attempt to speak to them *like* the gospel, in their language and putting myself in their place."[12] The distinction could be applied equally well to de Diétrich.

This combination of deep spirituality and keen intellectual awareness is unfortunately not a prominent feature of North American Protestantism, which tends toward one or the other quality but rarely combines the two. It is nevertheless a characteristic, and a vital one, of the Student Christian Movement as it was, at least, prior to the 1960s. Those of us who first acquired our theological eyeteeth within that movement, whether in Europe, Britain, Asia, Africa, or the New World, easily recognize behind the writings of Suzanne de Diétrich a type of Christianity for which most of us have the deepest respect—and in all likelihood (I can at least speak for myself) a certain nostalgia.[13] For while de Diétrich is an outstanding representative of that manner of living the faith, she was by no means unique. The S.C.M. was a remarkable movement precisely because it combined intellectual integrity and (in Bonhoeffer's sense) worldliness with an abiding curiosity about, and gratitude for, the biblical and doctrinal traditions of Christianity; thus, for countless students over several generations, the S.C.M. bridged the otherwise forbidding gap between the intellectual world of the academy and the confessional milieu of the churches. It is not accidental that de Diétrich not only found her faith and her vocation in the midst of this movement but herself shaped its destiny as a profound influence in the lives of many others.

Suzanne de Diétrich's approach to the scriptures can be summarized, I think, under three headings: critical reflection, exegetical imaginativeness, and nurture of the *koinonia*.

1. CRITICAL REFLECTION

"I was a skeptical young girl, who asked a lot of questions," wrote de Diétrich of her youth;[14] nor did her conversion imply "that all her skepticism and critical self-analysis had miraculously evaporated."[15] Her faith was faith, not credulity. Quite naturally, she approached the Bible with her critical acumen fully intact. With her early mentor Jules Breitenstein, a Reformed pastor and professor of New Testament, who like herself was "deeply committed to the biblical training of lay people,"[16] de Diétrich "was averse to any dogmatic stance which allowed no honest questioning of the biblical text."[17]

Not surprisingly, therefore, de Diétrich welcomed the historical-critical approach to scripture and continuously acquainted herself with the works of biblical scholars and commentators. In her book *Discovering the Bible,* she comments fairly extensively on historical criticism. Partly, she avers, it is "a reaction against an exclusively devotional approach to the Bible," and partly a Christian response to a wider scientific trend favoring the apparent objectivity of strict historical and linguistic research. One can already hear in this explanation intimations of both her appreciation and her criticism of the approach. On the side of appreciation, she writes:

> The attempt has been made to go back to the 'sources' behind the actual documents in our possession; the criteria being those of language, style, historical setting as well as actual content. Some of these investigations have been of a real scientific character. They have cleared up a number of linguistic difficulties and thus thrown new light on a number of obscure passages. They have helped to restore the historical setting in which certain events took place and have thus given new concreteness to the message delivered. They have made it possible for us to compare the Hebrew faith with neighbouring cultures and religions and thus enabled us to see more clearly in which its true originality consists. Last but not least, in reminding us that the writers of this book were subject like other authors to human and historical relativities, historical criticism has *saved us from any theories of verbal inspiration which would tend to substitute the external authority of a Book for the authority of the living God Who reveals Himself through this Book.*[18]

But de Diétrich's native skepticism was not about to bow down before the god of modern scholarship, any more than the deity of biblical literalism—especially, one might add with tongue slightly in cheek, scholarship originating in Germany! "An impartial study of the commentaries published in the last 50 or 60 years," she writes, "would show that the criteria on which a given author based his acceptance or rejection of a given text were very often grounded not on textual evidence but on the preconceived historical or philosophical theories of the author himself."[19] And we can readily imagine her reaction to the Jesus Seminar when we read:

Other schools have discarded as unauthentic any saying of Jesus in the Synoptic Gospels which sounded "Pauline." We could multiply such examples to show how assumptions of a quite different nature, namely, presuppositions of a dogmatic kind, have played into the picture and coloured a so-called scientific research.[20]

She was particularly critical of "the psychological approach," which she saw as "another pit into which the 'historical school' has sometimes fallen," for the "danger" here is that one approaches the Bible, "no longer in order to listen to what God has to say to us, but to analyse it as an anthology of moral and religious experiences. The *man* Jeremiah or the *man* Paul becomes the centre of the picture. . . . Have we not missed Paul's whole Gospel if our attention centres on Paul . . . ?"[21]

In sum, she considered the historical-critical approach "a blessing rather than a hindrance," but it fails if it draws too much attention to itself and detracts from the fundamental role of scripture in the life of the church. "[W]hat matters," she insists, "is not the historical accuracy of every detail of each story, or its authorship, but the will and purpose of God which is meant to be revealed through this story. We are faced with the two 'testaments' of this body of believers. Their claim is on our faith and our allegiance."[22]

If she issued a caveat to the exegetes, however, her warning to theologians with axes to grind is still stronger medicine:

We live in a time when certain words have become so secularized that we have lost sight of their Biblical meaning. This is the case of words such as "justice," "peace," "freedom." They have become slogans, tools of propaganda and party politics. Christians must know their true meaning in order not to fall prey to ideologies which use and misuse them. A thorough study of these words throughout the Bible will prove extremely fruitful and enriching.[23]

It is obvious to judicious readers of her work that Suzanne de Diétrich never relinquished a certain "hermeneutics of suspicion" where professional Christian scholarship was concerned. Some undoubtedly attributed this to her sensitivity as a nonprofessional (and a woman), but there is excellent justification for such caution both in scripture and in the Reformed tradition, whose emphasis on the sole sovereignty and glory *of God* precludes any pretentions to ultimacy by humans, and especially humans who claim familiarity with "the things of God."

There was, besides, a very *practical* reason why de Diétrich entertained a certain wariness of the scholars and why she herself never aspired to that role and reputation: she feared that too much Christian scholarship was undertaken for its own sake and not for the sake of the church—was indeed robbing the church of its access to its principal resource. And did she not have good cause to think so?

It was perhaps excessive—but was it not also consistent with the purity of her critique and her vocation as interpreter among the *laos*?—that she did not learn either Greek or Hebrew. When urged to do so,[24] she declined. Why? "She wanted to remain among the lay people. With the whole Bible before her, she remained passionately interested in the questions the world asks while listening to the questions and commands God addresses to politicians and teachers, to lawyers and labourers. Such simultaneous listening to the word and the world gave Suzanne a special prophetic discernment."[25]

---

2. INVOLVEMENT WITH THE TEXT AND EXEGETICAL IMAGINATIVENESS

Perhaps what bothered Suzanne de Diétrich about much modern biblical scholarship, besides its remote professionalism, was its captivation by what her countryman Jacques Ellul called "the great modern divinity, the Moloch of fact."[26] Granting the "immense contributions" of historical and linguistic studies of the scriptures over the past nearly two centuries, it remains that they only rarely (and with a few marvelous exceptions) produce in one what the Japanese theologian Masao Takenaka called the "A-ha!" experience—the experience of meaningful discovery.[27] In other words, one is enlightened without often being inspired. Information is imparted, and it is sometimes vital information, but it rarely grasps one or makes profound existential connections with one's life.

El Greco's painting of Saint Jerome, the original of which hangs in the Frick Gallery of New York City, depicts that ancient scholar poised before the Bible to whose translation and communication he devoted his life. His finger is pointing to a text—and his face betrays . . . conviction: he has been weighed in the balances and found wanting. Far from being a detached authority, he is a man *under* authority, judged by the authority under which he stands. It is this attitude and posture, one of passionate involvement, that Suzanne de Diétrich brings to her exegetical—or perhaps better, expositional—labors.

Consequently, her interpretation of the Bible—even in the small volumes that she left behind her, which, according to the testimony of many of her pupils, represents only a fraction of the interest that she communicated in her study groups—is full of imagination. It is not the kind of imagination that sets no limits to its flights of fantasy and substitutes spiritual immediacy for intellectual rigor. To the contrary. She believed that "the Bible is its own interpreter," that "[e]very part should be seen in the light of the whole,"[28] and that the first task of the student "is to find out what the text really means."[29] But finding that out—achieving real *knowledge* of the text—vastly transcends "research." Commitment is involved. "A non-commital attitude, an amateurish kind of intellectual curiosity will never lead us beyond an external knowledge of the Bible. Because we deal here not with an abstract system but with a living relationship, only through trust and commitment can we test the reality of this relationship."[30] In the words of one of her translators, Robert McAfee Brown, "the Bible *speaks to you*."[31] It is *the Bible* that speaks, and the first requirement of the student is to *listen*; but it speaks *to you*. And if you are to hear "hearingly" what it says, you will have to give yourself to it in all the specificity, honesty, and hiddenness of your being.

Given such pedagogical presuppositions, one is not surprised to find in de Diétrich's works insights and connections that have more in common with the exegetical writings of the Reformers (Luther, especially) than with most modern biblical scholarship. Partly, this can be traced to her conviction (as stated above) that the interpreter, though necessarily dealing always with the Bible's "parts," must do so as one conscious of and familiar with "the whole." She did not have modern biblical scholarship's inordinate fear of typologizing and similar holistic devices of the ancients that enable the interpreter to grasp internal connections in the testaments themselves—for example the juxtaposition of Pentecost (Acts 2) and Babel (Genesis 11).[32] But the greater reason for her exegetical insightfulness lies, I think, in her insistence upon reflective encounter between text and context—the social as well as the individual's own life situation, even to the point of betraying, on occasion, one's personal vulnerability.

The following commentary on Genesis 3, for example, could only have been written by someone with a great deal of exposure to her world, and with unrelenting self-knowledge, as well as acquired familiarity with the text:

God had made man to be "over against" him in responsibility. He made woman to be the companion "over against" the man. To them both he had entrusted the care of the created universe. In not accepting the destiny which God had given them, in wishing to be their own masters, these human beings have cut themselves off from God, and also from their neighbour. Henceforth they are like tops which spin round themselves; they twist and turn and knock against one another.

Humanity is going to become a world of spinning tops: each man thinks first of all of himself; little individual tops which prevent the creation of any real community. Big tops: one clan up in arms against the other; one power against another power. And all these turning round and round themselves in a closed circle. In detaching ourselves from God we have destroyed

love; we have destroyed all true liberty in human relationships.[33]

It will be said, perhaps, that this kind of writing is more sermon
than exegesis, but what is the point of exegesis if it does not trans-
late into sermon—address? Obviously de Diétrich could not live
with a text without knowing *herself* to be addressed by it—for example, these remarks on Luke 7:36ff.:

> He was able to break the chains of a poor woman whom the
> world labelled as "lost"; for him she was a human being, loved
> by God. In his whole attitude towards her he made her feel dig-
> nity as a woman; for the first time a man looked at her without
> lustful glances and without contempt; here, she began to real-
> ize, is "someone who believes that even for *me* there is a possi-
> bility of a new and pure life." Then her heart was full of
> gratitude and joy: "Jesus believes that there is a future for me!"
> And she in turn believed in him! And recognized in him One
> whom God had sent.[34]

There are also strong intimations of personal involvement in her
commentary on the text "where the Spirit of the Lord is, there is
liberty" (2 Corinthians 3), with the background of Galatians. The
titled Frenchwoman, who "remained only too well aware of the
disparity between her strong social consciousness and her relatively affluent situation,"[35] can be heard here contending with her
heritage—without allowing herself the luxury of lightly resolving
its paradoxes. Her struggle with privilege also, of course, entailed
lifelong efforts to distribute her wealth and its benefits responsibly, but this, and her personal modesty, did not answer the riddle
of inequality for her.[36] For her, the only answer worth contemplating was to be found in the gospel of freedom from self, freedom for life.

> What does this [liberty] mean, in practice—for my daily life?
> It means that I commit the past with its sins, its failures or
> successes to the Lord; that I am no longer the slave of my past;
> that I do not look back.
> This means that I can live fully in the present moment; taste

and enjoy all human joys as a gift which God gives to me, and endure all the sufferings and conflicts, because my Lord bears them with me.

This means that I can look forward to "tomorrow" without anxiety and without panic, for the Lord knows this unknown future; he has prepared it; and he will go through it with me.

Thus he communicates to me his own liberty, with regard to people, things, and circumstances. In him is given back to me the world with all the possibilities, all the riches, which the Creator has placed within it.

The liberty of the Christian allows him to enjoy without scruple, and intend with fresh intensity, all that the world offers that is beautiful and good.

But it also means that we are to use the things of this world as though they were not [1 Cor. 7:31]—that is to say, we can do without them when they are denied to us; for our real treasure is elsewhere.

That is the joyful liberty which the Lord wills to give even in this life to his own.[37]

---

3. NURTURE OF THE KOINONIA
AND WORLDLY ENGAGEMENT

Uppermost in the mind of this tireless leader of Bible study, however, is her conviction that the Christian community is dependent upon scripture both for its own life and for its worldly mission. She did not question the need for systematic theology, but she felt that the language of dogmatics and philosophic theology was increasingly inaccessible to the laity and encouraged a certain elitism. In an essay of 1971, she gave vent to some of her fears about the way academic theology seemed to be going, with its tendency to address the academy too exclusively and its loss of a biblical center.

She suggested we might be in a period where God remained silent, an experience which the prophets had long before us. For her the only way to come by a comprehensive view of Christian faith was to elaborate a new biblical theology through exegesis.

"I am deeply convinced that, because of its realistic and practical approach, the biblical view on human beings and on history, and even on God, is more accessible to many of our contemporaries than the often abstruse philosophical-theological theories we often offer them." Suzanne was implicitly alluding to the death-of-God theology which she had come across in the USA, and to ideologically conditioned views of Jesus as an existentialist or a Marxist which she encountered among students in France. Despite her great concern to draw out socio-political implications from the prophets and the gospel texts she consistently rejected a uni-dimensional reduction of the Bible to a political gospel.[38]

The "realistic and practical" character of the Bible did *not* mean, for her, that the Bible reduced everything to immediately comprehensible and self-evident precepts. "The Bible never offers ready-made answers to any of our questions. Because 'faith' is a dynamic, not a static reality, because we are always faced with the absolute of God's claim and calling on the one hand, and the world-as-it-is on the other, the full answer to any problem will always be paradoxical—thoroughly realistic, and yet charged with expectancy, the expectancy of faith, 'a firm conviction of things not seen,' yet already *given,* actual and real."[39]

As the last quotation makes plain, de Diétrich shared with all the others we have treated in this study a strong recognition of what Brunner named the "encounter" character of divine revelation, and therefore a refusal to reduce revelation to propositional truths. This entailed for her not only a struggle against intellectualism, dogma, and ideology, but against the greater temptation of the religious to contract discipleship to morality. The best antidote to that temptation, typical of so much North American Protestantism, is serious and sustained Bible study within the congregation. For the Bible is as much against moralism as it is against intellectualism. Its ethics are inseparable from its testimony to God.

Ethics and social ethics are never 'autonomous' in the Bible: we are not presented with an impersonal code of morals valid for all times, but with a living God Whose claim to obedience is always concrete. Of course commandments are laid down (the ten commandments, for instance); but they are compelling because of Him who speaks them, the saving God: 'I am the Lord thy God which have brought thee out of the land of Egypt, out of the house of bondage.' Never can the law be separated from the Law-giver.[40]

Anticipating a later theological emphasis, particularly among feminist authors, de Diétrich explains the inseparability of gospel and law in the language of relationality:

The Bible thinks in terms of relationship and God's relationship with us sets the pace (if we may say so) for our relationships with one another. . . . Biblical ethics are not static but dynamic because they are at every moment a concrete obedience flowing out of our relationship with the living God, of our belonging to the community of His beloved.[41]

To those accustomed to approaching the Bible as scholars and researchers, de Diétrich's concern for Bible study among the laity and nonprofessionals, including her detailed and careful suggestions about how such study ought to be conducted, may seem remarkable—even perhaps naive. Clearly, as her biographer points out, "Suzanne's vocation was that of the Bible study animator and not that of the biblical researcher." As such, he continues, she was not unaware of her limitations: "She knew that an animator risks becoming a manipulator when neglecting the biblical texts, and the messages such texts address to readers are lost sight of. Therefore she always remained a student, keenly interested in what was happening in biblical scholarship."[42]

But de Diétrich's work and example accomplish something that more specialized biblical study rarely achieves—even, one suspects, when it is successful in touching the students of theology who become the church's ministers. De Diétrich restores the Word of God to the people of God. Unless and until the Bible becomes the church's workbook, the whole point of Reformation Protestantism will be dissipated—at least the point of Protestantism, if not the church as a whole. Scholarship both theological and exegetical *can*, if it will, aid this process, but it remains for those who are ready to risk their professional reputations for wholeness and the stewardship of wisdom to carry their passion for understanding to the pews and to the streets and to the centers of intellectual life.

Conclusions

In a remarkable essay for the Kegley and Bretall festschrift for Emil Brunner,[1] Wilhelm Pauck discusses the theological movement that dominated the first part of the present century in the broad historical context of Christianity in the modern period. He finds that these theologians, the most prominent of whom he regards as Barth, Brunner, Bultmann, Nygren, Tillich, and Reinhold Niebuhr, were responding on the one hand to the breakdown of Western Christendom and on the other to the incapacity of both the old orthodoxies and their own liberal mentors creatively to address the post-Christendom situation. Their work was evoked by the inability of liberal Christianity in particular to speak to the crisis of civilization starkly revealed by the outbreak of World War I but already presaged in the testimony of the greatest seers of the nineteenth century: Kierkegaard, Marx, Nietzsche, and Freud.

Compelled, after 1918, to break with the liberalism by which they had been formed, these theologians, writes Pauck, "all became 'neo-orthodox' or were so labelled by their critics." Some of them "should never have been called neo-orthodox, Tillich and Bultmann, for example. Others were in fact never neo-orthodox, theologically speaking: Reinhold Niebuhr, for instance."[2] Their work manifests nothing like "unanimity" either at its beginning or in its development. Yet they are all participants in a distinctive theological movement and can be considered such especially in their common absorption with "five large themes."[3]

1. REVELATION

Over against the decision of theological liberalism from Schleiermacher onward to base theology on human religious consciousness, the new theology interpreted the Christian faith on the basis of God's revelatory Word in Jesus Christ. Thus, "[i]nstead of asking: What has modern man to say about the gospel? The theologians now concerned themselves with the question: What does the gospel say to modern man?"[4] And in this connection, one finds in these theologians:

2. A NEW EMPHASIS ON THE BIBLE

"It must be called 'new,'" Pauck insists, "in contrast to the traditionalist *and* the modernist views of the Bible."

> It is a view of the Bible different from that which can be obtained by the use of the historical method for the interpretation of historical texts and documents, because it takes the books of the Bible as the bearers of a kerygma, a message of salvation that must be believed. On the other hand, it has nothing in common with the view of the fundamentalists, who stress the literal inerrancy of the Bible as if this were the foremost article of the Christian faith.[5]

It is understood that the kerygma, "the gospel of Christ," represents "a scandal and a provocation" to the contemporary world, but this is not because the primary witness to this kerygma is a collection of ancient manuscripts. Rather, it is because of the radical message of the cross as such, calling in question, as it does, human efforts at self-salvation and offering human beings "renewal through the forgiveness of sins." "This view," Pauck declares, "is basically that of all the theologians we have named, but they present it in different ways.[6]

3. HISTORICAL CONSCIOUSNESS

All the theologians concerned, says the historian Pauck, have been profoundly influenced by the liberalism that they criticize, and nowhere more obviously than in their recognition that all theology is historically conditioned. The church possesses no transhistorical or suprahistorical truth, no eternal theology, but is called to bear witness to the gospel in its own time and place and according to the (always-limited) wisdom vouchsafed to it. In this, writes Pauck, "liberal theology, which [the new theology] censures so strictly in many parts, nevertheless is allowed to live on." "This," Pauck continues, "is as it ought to be—for it is impossible for any modern interpreter of Christianity to think in any other historical terms."[7] (We may add that what today we would call contextuality in theology is indeed a legacy of liberalism—and a powerful one.)

4. INFLUENCE OF THE REFORMATION

"What would neo-orthodoxy in all its shades and shadings be without the Luther-and-Calvin Renaissance which has been going on now for more than a generation and which has made it possible for the great Protestant Reformers to speak in their own name as they have not been able to do in any previous period of Protestant history?" None of the theologians under discussion is simply a Lutheran or a Calvinist, Pauck rightly observes; indeed, "denominational loyalty" has nothing to do with it. But all of them are "under the sway" of the great reformers, especially (in his view) Luther.[8]

5. ECUMENICAL CHARACTER

That the theology in question is "ecumenical in character and outlook" does not refer only to the active involvement of its leading representatives in the ecumenical movement, but chiefly to the way in which they do theology. None of these theologians, Pauck notes, "think and speak on behalf of the particular denomination to which he happens to belong and none chooses to deny his denominational home in any way (for the simple reason, in the last resort, that no man can jump out of his skin!), but every one of them addresses himself as a theological interpreter of Christianity *to Christians everywhere and to all sorts and conditions of men.*" [9]

I have summarized Wilhelm Pauck's five common themes in some detail because I have found no better generalization about the character of this theological movement. What seems to me particularly commendable (and it is not independent of the fact that Pauck was a historian) is that, in naming these *common* motifs, he has avoided on the one hand the narrowness of confining "neo-orthodoxy" to one particular thinker or school (Barth, usually) and on the other hand has left plenty of room for shadings and differences within the movement as a whole. In what follows, I shall make generous use of all five of these themes.

Two of these motifs, however, need further elaboration if they are to achieve their full significance for us today. The first is implicit in Pauck's first "large theme," and to some extent in the second and third as well, but as it appears, even in the original, of which I have quoted only segments, it is easily overlooked. Speaking of the revelatory basis of the movement, Pauck writes that it centers in "the knowledge of God which is guided by the acknowledgment of God's disclosure of himself in Christ."[10] And in the second place, in connection with the "new Biblicism," he stresses that it is "oriented to the *message* of the Bible, the gospel of Christ."[11] What needs to be added to this if the point is not to be lost is that there is reasserted here, over against liberalism's anthropocentrism, a *working Christocentrism* that is determinative for both Christian theology and Christian anthropology; moreover—and this seems to me especially important, for otherwise such Christocentrism could be mistaken for yet another revival of conservative orthodoxy—the Christ who is at the center of the revelatory event to which the Bible bears primary witness is the nontriumphalistic, kenotic, crucified Christ, whose glory is "hidden beneath its opposite" (Luther).

It is far from incidental, then, that the reformer most frequently sought out by these theologians (Barth's later and avowed adherence to Calvin notwithstanding) is Martin Luther (part of Pauck's fourth theme). Nor is it incidental that *all* the major figures in this story, albeit in differing ways but in ways that are recognizably related, articulate their accounts of the Christian message as contemporary expressions of the *theologia crucis,* and therefore as ongoing critiques of both orthodox and liberal versions of the theology of glory (*theologia gloriae*). In some (for example, the early Barth, Bultmann, Tillich, Bonhoeffer) this continuity with the "thin tradition" that Luther named "theology of the cross" is explicit and deliberate; in others (especially Reinhold Niebuhr, who, as we noted earlier, never used the term "theology of the cross") it is implicit and intuitive. But it is unmistakably present in all the major manifestos of this movement, even when (as in the case of the later Barth) there is a certain apprehension of turning this, too, into another ideology.

Since I have discussed this theological tradition in many other places,[12] I shall not expatiate on the import of this underlying theme for a right understanding of this whole movement. If, however, as Jürgen Moltmann beautifully expresses it,[13] the theology of the cross is not simply a chapter in theology but the "key signature" of the whole enterprise, and if precisely this neglected and "unloved" (Moltmann) tradition is of the essence of what these theologians have picked up and articulated in contemporary terms, then it must be said to be of the greatest significance in their common witness. I repeat: they are not just committed to Jesus Christ in some general way; they are committed to an account of the Christ, and therefore of all else, that takes with utter seriousness the cross that is at the center of the biblical testimony to the Christ. Whether systematically or indirectly and thematically, they all attempt to articulate *the whole tradition* from the perspective of this center. Tillich's words at the end of his *The Courage to Be* could be endorsed, I think, by every one of these thinkers:

[A] church which raises itself in its message and its devotion to the God above the God of theism without sacrificing its concrete symbols can mediate a courage which takes doubt and meaninglessness into itself. It is the Church under the Cross which alone can do this, the Church which preaches the Crucified who cried to God who remained his God after the God of confidence had led him in the darkness of doubt and meaninglessness. To be as a part in such a church is to receive the courage to be in which one cannot lose one's self and in which one receives one's world.[14]

The second motif that Pauck has—not omitted, certainly, but—developed insufficiently concerns the audience for which these authors are conscious of doing their work of discernment and edification. This is hinted at, perhaps, in the fifth theme, but without further elaboration it would be greatly understated. Perhaps the missing point was not so obvious in 1962 when this essay was published, but today it cannot be missed by any attentive reader of these authors—namely, that all of them manifest *a strong sense of responsibility toward the whole church.*

One does not mean by this an exclusively ecclesiastical orientation, of course. Hardly! These theologians are all (not least the most kerygmatic of them: Barth, the writer of *Church Dogmatics*) *public* theologians, intent upon addressing, as Pauck says, "all sorts and conditions of men." But they all—even Tillich, who as apologist cast his net most widely—interpret their vocation as teachers of the church, the *whole* church, and what Pauck rightly identifies as their "ecumenicity" stems directly from that vocational orientation.

It is not accidental, in this respect, that so many of them were Christian pastors and ministers before they became professional teachers and writers of theology, nor is it accidental that nearly all of them were, or became, educators in Christian theological seminaries and faculties. In every instance, they set themselves the task of interpreting the whole message of the Christ to the whole church.

And in this connection more than any other, this movement, by whatever name it may be called, differentiates itself from most of what came after it, which is undoubtedly why this particular common motif is more conspicuous today than it was in 1962.

How shall we speak of "what came after it"? We could notice, for instance, that in contrast to the aforementioned observation that theological discourse during the first part of this century was largely determined by individuals who were pastors and seminary professors, since the 1960s much of the most prominent theological discourse has been profoundly influenced by scholars not directly, or only indirectly, responsible to churches. This is particularly the case in North America. With the opening up of "religious studies" in a great many secular institutions formerly suspicious of religion, and the consequent possibility of earning one's living as a teacher of religion independently of any confessional allegiance, many who might otherwise have sought careers within Christian educational institutions have found their vocations in secular colleges and faculties—that is, in situations where confessionalism is usually discouraged and upfront belief as such often frowned upon. Moreover, partly through the impact of the creative work of these new professionals and partly because of the growing religious plurality of our social context, the influence of "religious studies" has by no means confined itself to the secular academy but has spread into the theological colleges and seminaries of the churches as well; so that, not only in biblical studies but in systematic theology and ethics too there has been in mainline Protestant educational centers in North America (as distinct from Europe) a certain pressure to accentuate objectivity and research and to be wary of a too belief-ful orientation to one's subject matter.

Whether one regards all this positively or negatively, it cannot, I think, be gainsaid that since the mid-1960s Christian theology has been far more academic than it was during the previous decades of the century. By comparison with the persons treated in the foregoing chapters of this book, I venture to suggest, relatively few members of the present cohort of teachers of theology feel themselves to be more immediately responsible to the community of faith than to the academy. Indeed, if a comparison were made between the articles published in the leading religious journals of the past and those of today, it would be noted, I am sure, that present-day scholars write for their various guilds and for one another far more frequently than they speak as "interpreters of Christianity [addressing themselves] to Christians everywhere and to all sorts and conditions of men" (Pauck).

It will be pointed out—and rightly so—that this trend toward detached professionalism and academic theology has been and is countered, however, by another prominent trend in Christian theology since the 1960s: that is, the advent of theological movements and concerns growing out of intensive involvement with some particular element of society or some cluster of problems or special issues. It could hardly be said of such movements as black theology, Christian feminism, gay and lesbian concerns, solidarity with indigenous peoples or ethnic groupings, ecological or peace or justice issues, and so on that they are productive of purely academic approaches to Christian theology! Indeed, the opposite charge is the usual one: that they are far too involved.

Speaking for myself, I welcome the involvement and support it wherever possible! It is in my opinion entirely preferable to the quest for an allegedly value-free approach and the substitution of bloodless research for depth of commitment and reflection. Moreover, far from being a merely personal preference, I take this to be a necessity implicit within the Christian theological discipline itself; for the object that this theology seeks to understand and articulate is, as Karl Barth insisted, no object but a living Subject. Even the academy must recognize (and it regularly claims to do so!) that the method appropriate to any discipline is determined by the nature of its content. And for all the absurd reductionism rampant in the modern university, with everyone trying to mimic the methodology of the hard sciences (after all, they acquire most of the grants), Christian theology betrays and distorts its subject matter when it pursues the objectifiable *aspects* of the disciplines as if they represented its core. (And it is beginning to be clear, or clearer, that this is as true of *biblical* studies as of systematics and ethics.[15])

This right and necessary practice of deep involvement, however, does not obviate the particular problem toward which, in these observations, I am moving: namely, the problem of detachment from the *whole church*—or, to put it in terms of the vocational orientation of the theologian, the problem that arises when theological communities regard their primary responsibility as being directed toward some specific grouping or issue within or around the whole as differentiated from "Christians everywhere and all sorts and conditions of men."

It will help to clarify this point if we consider the same *kind* of problem as it manifests itself in the public sphere at large. Many observers of contemporary American and Canadian society concern themselves with the tendency of perhaps the most engaged and vigilant social critics and activists to deflect concern for the whole public sphere by too-exclusive preoccupation with particular groups or issues. For example, Jean Bethke Elshtain argues that democracy itself is "on trial" when its most important category, that of citizenship, gives way to "the politics of difference."

> [O]ur own democracy—I speak here as an American—is faltering, not flourishing. More and more, we Americans confront one another as aggrieved groups rather than as free citizens.[16]

Or again:

> To the extent citizens begin to retribalize into ethnic or other "fixed-identity groups," democracy falters. Any possibility for human dialogue, for democratic communication and

commonality, vanishes as so much froth on the polluted sea of phony equality. Difference more and more becomes exclusivist. If you are black and I am white by definition I do not and cannot, in principle, "get in."[17]

Mistrust and cynicism born of fierce loyalties to group identity erode the foundational concept of "civil society," that is, society "as a realm that is neither individualist nor collectivist" but "partakes of both the 'I' and the 'we.'"[18]

Repudiating the "sameness" of equality for its homogenizing urge, difference ideologues embrace their own version of sameness—an exclusionist sameness along lines of gender, race, ethnicity, and sexual preference. . . . This tendency leads to a terrible impasse . . . , one to which "the politics of difference and the ideology of multiculturalism have contributed by rendering suspect the language of collectivity, common action, and shared purposes."[19]

Another author is especially concerned about the decimations that this tendency visits upon the most *critically* vigilant element in our society, the political Left. Todd Gitlin, author of *The Twilight of Common Dreams: Why America Is Wracked by Culture Wars,* argues that the Left, to which he himself evidently belongs, "has fragmented into what he calls 'identity politics,' where distinct subgroups, based on race, gender, sexuality, ethnicity or disability, fight on behalf of their own needs." The emergence of these groups, he believes, has been understandable and necessary, and there can be no doubt that advocacy of their situations and rights by marginalized groups has "improved their positions in recent decades." These gains, however, are not to be had without a lamentable cost: in splintering into separate pockets of "identity," the Left has been desperately weakened and its "common cause" (as glimpsed in the counterculture of the 1960s) "abandoned." As a result, unnecessary and humanly dangerous political victories have been ceded to the Right.[20]

It is not my purpose here to ask how Christians ought to respond to this kind of social analysis or the realities that it depicts; I only wish to suggest that a situation very similar, and, obviously enough, inseparable from the general societal picture, pertains within the mainline Protestant community in the United States and Canada; there, too, concern for the whole has, in the past three or four decades, given way to preoccupation with specific parts of the community and to those aspects of the gospel that seem most directly to address the parts. To the "identity politics" of the greater social sphere there corresponds in and around these denominations a cluster of identity theologies that, in their effect if not always according to their intentions, detract from vital concern for the whole Christian movement.

But before I proceed along these lines, let me assure the reader: It is far from my intention to insinuate that theologies emerging out of the various identities and issues concerned are in themselves and as such either wrong or avoidable. To the contrary. It has been absolutely necessary in the Christian community for oppressed and marginalized groups and submerged issues to come to the fore. Christianity was not only impoverished without their witness, it was culpable in their marginalization. Potentially, and to some extent actually, the critical rethinking of the faith undertaken by these groupings *does* contribute to the whole by introducing into the dialogue of the ages voices and concerns that were not heard—that ought, according to the gospel basis of this faith, to have been heard all along!

But, in my view and at least until the present, this potential for enrichment of the whole has not occurred significantly—partly because the most dominant ecclesiastical elements, numerically speaking, have ignored or rejected this testimony, and partly because the identity- and issue-groupings themselves have been too self-absorbed, exclusionary, and distrustful of the churches to make more than a superficial and usually only a programatic difference.

The pathos of this is rightly and pointedly identified by Gitlin:

paralleling the larger political scene, when the critical cutting edge of the Christian movement (the Christian Left, if you will) falters and fragments into identity- and issue-theologies, victory is ceded to the most reactionary (Right) elements within the churches. "Neo-orthodoxy" was capable of confronting and challenging the religious conservativism that is somehow native to North America, and especially to the United States, because it concerned itself with the basics of the whole tradition and the future of the whole church. And let us not mistake it: it did so as a movement of the Left, thus understood. I have been at pains to demonstrate that fact in all seven of the foregoing chapters. If the term "neo-orthodoxy" was and is a misnomer and, indeed, a put-down, it is because it falsely attributes to this movement a mere return to reactionary, predictable orthodoxy, and in this way takes the sting out of this movement. This was a *critical* theological movement, critical simultaneously and equally of old orthodoxies, genuine or ersatz, and of nineteenth-century liberalism and modernism; critical as much in its constructive as in its deconstructive labors. The *great* legacy of so-called neo-orthodoxy is in fact just this critical—let me say more explicitly, this *prophetic*—role. And this is precisely and chiefly the legacy that *has not been claimed.*

Obviously I do not mean that *no one* has taken up that role—such a blanket judgment would be absurd. But I do mean that the legacy of prophetic witness to the *church* as a whole, on the part of persons struggling with the *tradition* as a whole, has not been where theology in North America since the 1960s has expended its energies. The main theological emphases of the past few decades have in fact been so lacking in concern for the whole people of God, so preoccupied with deconstruction of the tradition, and so divided into parts that are themselves unconnected and often at loggerheads, that at the level of theological *foundations* mainline Protestant Christianity in North America exists in an unprecedented state of confusion. On questions of basic belief, congregations untouched by serious theology revert to opinions and prejudices that have not changed for a hundred years and more. And the reversion is even more pathetic when it comes to questions of morality.

As I noted in passing in connection with H. Richard Niebuhr's Christology, this situation was again brought home for us recently in Canada when the moderator of the largest mainline Protestant denomination, the United Church of Canada, made certain remarks about "the divinity of Christ" that touched off a flashy religious controversy. Surprisingly, given the generally secular mentality of my country, the controversy blossomed into a full-scale media event, at the height of which the most popular national magazine, *MacLean's,* devoted its lead article to the question, "Is Jesus Really God?"[21] The question itself sounds like a replay of past history, but the answers to it, provided both by religious leaders and the general, once-Christian public, were such that an informed person could only conclude that nothing significant in Christian theology had occurred since the modernists and fundamentalists battled it out in 1895. To the injured declaration of fundamentalists and the self-declared orthodox that Jesus certainly *is* God (a declaration already called in question by Chalcedon!), liberal churchfolk predictably accentuated his human example and teachings. At no time in the debate did I hear anything that sounded as if it might have been informed, even at second hand, by Paul Tillich, Karl Barth, or any of the others we have considered here — *nor,* indeed, by representatives of any of the major theological schools since 1960.

In saying this, I am of course indicting "neo-orthodoxy" itself, and not only its various successors — the by-now long line of "theologies of." For of course the question must be asked, *Why did not "neo-orthodoxy" itself beget a more committed and imaginative progeny?* If it held, as one of its most vital common themes, the nurture and empowering of the ecumenical church; if this is indeed, as I have argued, of the very essence of its "legacy," how is it to be explained that this movement did not create in subsequent generations cohorts of theologians and church leaders sufficiently inspired by its witness to want to claim precisely this legacy?

To be sure, individual names can be brought forward at this point, and some of them really do qualify as inheritors of this tradition of prophetic scholarship and concern. (I make no secret of the fact that I should like to number myself among them!) But I do not have the evidence to demonstrate that the labors and intentions of this movement, as they are insightfully summarized in Wilhelm Pauck's common themes, were transferred to subsequent generations of theological and ecclesiastical leadership with enough internal compulsion to lay claim to the legacy of the movement itself. In none of the five large themes—revelation, Bible, historical consciousness, continuity with the Reformation, and ecumenical orientation—has theology since 1960 manifested in its overall performance anything like an apostolic continuity with this movement.

And in this respect it has to be concluded, I think, that at least in North America "neo-orthodoxy" itself must be said to have failed. If it ever commanded more than a minority influence, it did not make a lasting impression. What remains of it in our context has too consistently channeled itself into theological programs and causes that betray both its wholeness and its radicality: for example, a Barthianism that embraces the orthodoxy that is present in Barth without appropriating any of Barth's radical restatement of orthodoxy nor (especially!) his socialist politics; or, a Tillichianism that embraces Tillich's cultural and religious openness without noticing the christological foundations of that openness; or a Niebuhrianism that loves Reinhold Niebuhr's sense of the "ambiguity" of all human behavior without emulating Niebuhr's ethical boldness in the pursuit of "proximate goals."

Why did "neo-orthodoxy" fail in North America? The answer must be complex, and even the most complex answer will not fully explain the situation, for it reflects the mystery of our very being as a people. For one thing, Christendom in North America has been and, in the United States, still is too entrenched to require, let alone welcome, any radical theological renewal. As the fate of Kierkegaard demonstrated long ago, churches that can seem to be successful without any depth of theological awareness are very likely to suspect and reject any theology that probes to the roots of both cultic and cultural convention. Combined with the anti-intellectualism characteristic of so much of our Protestantism, this vigilance against anything that would disturb the status quo was bound to resist a theology that raises fundamental questions about the whole functioning of religion in this society and encourages a faith that inculcates an abiding suspicion of power.

Again, the great crises that gave birth to this theology were either less dramatic or less visible in North America. While two World Wars and the Cold War have certainly colored our history, neither Americans nor Canadians experienced the immediate devastations of modern warfare, nor have we lived in such proximity to the communist alternative as to feel profoundly, its ultimate failure notwithstanding, the full impact of its critique of both religion and capitalism. As for the economic crisis that evoked the radical Christianity of the Detroit pastor Reinhold Niebuhr, or the racial crisis that raised up Martin Luther King Jr., the dominant culture of this society has been powerful enough to absorb and deflect these challenges to its rectitude and, moreover, to exploit the Christian religion to that end.

Still, another reason why this theology did not take root in our soil, it seems to me, is that theological liberalism, which in its broadest expressions dominated the Protestant mainstream, and which the new theology could most readily expect to influence, proved itself to be far stronger and more in tune with the aspirations of our middle classes than was the case in Europe. Indeed, religious liberalism and the middle class are still almost synonymous entities in this society, and that means, not only that the middle classes manifest a predictable preference for broad, nonspecific, and "nice" expressions of the Christian religion, but that they expect their religious leadership to teach and embody, personally, the virtues and values that they rhetorically cherish.

One consequence of these expectations (one that should not be overlooked in this connection) is that theological education of the clergy, even where it was inspired by this movement, was at a loss to find in denominational parishes an atmosphere supportive of such theological struggles. Many hundreds of ministerial candidates who were, as students, deeply moved by their exposure to the giants of this movement, were quickly absorbed into the general milieu of religious well-being as soon as they found themselves ministers of successful middle-class congregations. They might cite the names of Bonhoeffer or Tillich or Bultmann in their sermons, but as soon as they tried (as some did) to implement aspects of the teaching of such theologians (for example Bonhoeffer's theology of political resistance, or Barth's theology of baptism, or Niebuhr's critique of moralism) they invariably found themselves in trouble with their parishioners.

The failure of theological educators to communicate a lively and lasting passion for theology to their ministerial students is of course an old story, and as such it betokens some very serious questions about theological education as such. But in the case of this particular theological movement something else is at issue besides superficial or inadequate pedagogy. And here we return to the earlier observation that at the core of this movement there is a reappearance, in contemporary dress, of the *theologia crucis*. For how could young clerics, insufficiently introduced to these theologians in the first place, be expected to understand them profoundly, let alone perform the difficult integrative tasks necessary to making their teachings their own—*and* to do so in a sustained and creative way in the face of congregations, most of whom are inherently and intensely *opposed* to just these emphases? Christocentrism, and even Christomonism, does not go against the grain of North American cultus and culture when, whether in liberal or conservative forms, it serves to confirm our dominant culture in the rightness of its values and the triumph of *its* "way"—which triumphant Christology regularly does! But a Christocentrism that calls in question the culture of success, the religion of progress, and the whole apparatus of our rhetorical optimism; a biblically sensitive and historically informed Christology that refuses to lend Jesus Christ to ecclesiastical self-promotionalism and the cult of winning; a theology of radical grace that names the shallowness of moralism and offers forgiveness and reconciliation to the broken and ostracized (and all of this, and more, is what the theology of the cross is and does) does not endear itself to our way of life or to the scramble for "bourgeois transcendence" (Käsemann). Thus the deepest explanation for the failure of this theological movement in North America must be located precisely here—in its utter discontinuity with the religion that has been our most indigenous quest and preference.

But . . . just that religion, that "old theology," is today growing exceedingly threadbare. In a way that was simply not true in the 1950s, when "neo-orthodoxy" was at its most vigorous even in North America, triumphalism in both religion and society fails to convince the perceptive, and even the unperceptive are intuitively skeptical. Public cynicism dogs the rhetorical claims of the *imperium* to ever greater strength and an ever more glorious future.[22] Religious triumphalism of the most depthless and fatuous sort—the sort that can be reduced to television entertainment—has flown to the Christian Right, which once had to live outside our dominant culture but now aligns itself with empire. In this tawdry attire, the theology of glory shows itself the poor, deceptive thing that it has always been (Heidelberg Thesis 21!).[23]

In the meantime, the remnants of classical Protestantism—the once-mainline denominations—have suffered losses of membership, finances, and influence in high places. The bravado that characterized their life in the 1950s, the age of church building and important pulpits, has quite gone out of them—of course, with exceptions. Their people no longer know what to believe or how, as

Christians, they should act. Half-hearted if sometimes noisy efforts at church growth and spiritual renewal are undertaken, but how can anyone become excited about growing or being renewed if they are no longer confident of what it is that they are called upon to promote and inculcate?

What does this "humiliation" of once-proud Christendom, North American style, portend? How should it be interpreted by the Christianly serious?

One answer, and the only one worth contemplating, is that it portends a new possibility for Protestant Christianity—precisely the *kind* of biblically literate, historically conscious, socially responsible, christologically centered Christianity that "neo-orthodoxy" tried to introduce into our then-inhospitable soil. I do not dare to suggest that the soil is now, at the end of the century, positively receptive to this seed. Hardly! While Christendom has been busy falsely promoting and actually demeaning itself on this continent, religious plurality has blossomed and secularism has grown apace. There can be no attempt on the part of Christians who have noted the immense historical blunders and downright evils of Christendom over sixteen centuries to revive that Humpty-Dumpty! From now on, we are speaking of a diaspora when we speak of the church of Jesus Christ.

But it can be a faithful and a creative diaspora—salt, yeast, and light in a society vastly in need of these. It can be a Christian movement more vital, and more continuous with its pre-Constantinian beginnings, than nearly everything produced by centuries of Christian imperialism and chauvinism. It can inherit the best traditions of the past, especially of the Reformation, without the accompanying liabilities, most of which were direct consequences of the insidious quest for power and glory.

It can do all this, however, only if the great insights of the Reformers and their later disciples, including these same "neo-orthodox" theologians, are truly and imaginatively transmitted to *the whole people.* And here we ought to recognize, I think, that the nomenclature "neo-orthodox" is not *entirely* misleading.[24] For what these theologians were searching for was in a real sense nothing more than new ways of articulating and communicating sound teaching, the essence of the faith separated from the husks of its historical expressions—which is after all the root meaning of "orthodox." They were not out to repeat past orthodoxies, even the orthodoxies of the Reformers they usually (but by no means always) admired and quoted. They searched the scriptures and traditions for a gospel that would address their "today"—which is the only legitimate kind of gospel.

They were better at articulating that gospel, however, than at *communicating* it—in part because they were (as we have seen) in advance of their time and out of kilter with their religious constituencies, but in part, also, their failure as communicators was caused by certain problems inherent in their own enterprise. One way of indicating these problems is to note that they were still men of social standing, imbued with most of the ambitions of their class, glad of the rewards that their society bestowed still even on *Christian* intellectuals: nearly all of them, as we have noted earlier, had their pictures on the covers of *Time* and other leading magazines. A simpler way of saying this—but it is too simple, really—is to note that they were nearly all *men,* so far as the front lines of the movement are concerned.

While the masculine domination of the movement should not be overemphasized, it may certainly be asked whether a greater feminine presence might not have added both sensitivity and realism—sensitivity to the problems and possibilities of communication, and realism about church and society. One often has the impression, reading the works of these eminent theologians, that they haven't the least notion of how theologically impoverished and spiritually destitute both church and society were. They had to do chiefly with the more promising elements of both—the people who read their books and invited them to speak. Is it perhaps more than a little suggestive that, of the seven persons discussed in this study, the one who made the greatest effort to *communicate* the insights, particularly the biblical orientation, of this movement to ordinary people, and to the point of positively denying herself the symbols and accoutrements of intellectual prestige, was a woman? I do not say that Suzanne de Diétrich was alone in seeking to do this (that would be patently insupportable), but all too few of the most prominent (and therefore male) leaders of this movement made it their business to address the *laity,* whose importance, in theory, they certainly upheld, and few were very successful, in their academic settings, in inculcating in their undergraduate ministerial students the kind of biblical and theological excitement that the petite Alsatian baroness managed to inspire among generations of nonministerial university students. There was, as there still is, a great and gaping hiatus between what transpires in the theological classroom and what occurs in church pulpits and parlors. While the leaders of this movement had no power to change the atmosphere of churchly smugness and vacuousness that was present in mid-century American Protestantism, they must, surely, be held somewhat accountable for their seeming unawareness of this hiatus and their failure to overcome it at least from the side of the church's "teaching elders."

Now, at the end of "the Christian century," the smugness of cultural Christianity has conspicuously abated, except where quantitative success masks essential emptiness, and there is a certain readiness—even amounting here and there to hunger and thirst—for "solid food." This presents disciplined and serious-minded Protestant Christians, I have claimed, with new opportunities; not opportunities for grandeur and certainly not for worldly power and prestige, but for truth and wisdom. And for hope! The movement called "neo-orthodoxy" very incisively and perceptively exemplified for us the ways in which *those* opportunities can be grasped. The five large themes named by Wilhelm Pauck set forth these ways with singular accuracy and brevity: the revelatory, christological basis of the gospel; the indispensability of the study of the scriptures; keen and informed historical consciousness; an internalized and nuanced appropriation of the Reformation traditions in particular; and the attempt to address the whole church in the context of its real world. These are still the requirements of any who would take up the legacy, not only of this particular Protestant renewal, but of Protestant Christianity as a whole. Without these, mainline Protestantism will simply atrophy, dwindle, or be absorbed into existing forms of "religion," some of them noisily proclaiming themselves Protestant.

The point, however, is not merely to laud and magnify the thought of these giants of our immediate past, but to emulate their spirit — as the divine Spirit gives us the courage and imagination to do so in our substantially different time and place, and to do so with some realism about their limitations and failings. We are not called upon to say what they said, but to do what they did — and therefore I frankly mistrust the enthusiastic announcements of some at the end of this age that the great theologians of the twenty-first century are going to be Karl Barth, or Paul Tillich, or Dietrich Bonhoeffer. Not one of these theologians, human and prideful as they may have been, would for a moment endorse such vain prolongation of their names and fames! That they may and should *teach* us still has been the whole premise of this book. But *what* they teach us, in the end, should not and must not be to memorize and mimic their fondest thoughts, but to be and become, in our own time and our own place, committed and disciplined and above all *thoughtful* witnesses to the grace of God in Jesus Christ.

Notes

Introduction

1. Karl Barth, *How I Changed My Mind,* with an introduction and epilogue by John D. Godsey (Richmond: John Knox Press, 1966), 50.
2. Ibid., 62.
3. Most recently in Douglas John Hall, *The End of Christendom and the Future of Christianity* (Valley Forge, Pa.: Trinity Press International, 1997), and *Professing the Faith: Christian Theology in a North American Context,* vol. 3 of my trilogy (Minneapolis: Fortress Press, 1996).
4. H. Martin Rumscheidt, s.v. "neo-orthodoxy," in *Encyclopedia of the Reformed Faith,* ed. Donald E. McKim (Louisville, Ky.: Westminster John Knox Press, and Edinburgh: Saint Andrew Press, 1992), 253.
5. John Godsey, s.v. "neo-orthodoxy," in *Encyclopedia of Religion,* ed. Mircea Eliade (New York: Macmillan Publishing Co., 1986), 10:360ff.
6. Colin Brown, s.v. "neoorthodoxy," in *New International Dictionary of the Christian Church,* cd. J. D. Douglas (Grand Rapids: Zondervan Publishing House, 1974).
7. R. V. Schnucker, s.v. "neo-orthodoxy," in *Evangelical Dictionary of Theology,* ed. Walter A. Elwell (Grand Rapids: Baker Book House, 1984), 697.
8. For example, Alister E. McGrath says of "neo-orthodoxy" that it is "a term used to designate the general position of Karl Barth" (*The Christian Theology Reader* [Oxford: Basil Blackwell Publisher, 1994], 403).
9. I have not included here a discussion of Rudolf Bultmann. That is partly because I do not feel competent to survey his work, and partly because, like Oscar Cullmann and many other *biblical* scholars, Bultmann's contribution to this whole renewal of theology and church derives from a field of investigation that has its own method

and approach. I am, however, in complete agreement with Wilhelm Pauck when he considers Bultmann one of the foremost contributors to the "neo-orthodox" revival (see my Conclusions).

10. Besides those to whom chapters of this book are devoted, one could include such names as Gustaf Aulén, Friedrich Gogarten, Georges Casalis, W. A. Visser 't Hooft, Oscar Cullmann, Anders Nygren, Helmut Thielicke, D. T. Niles, Martin Niemöller, Ellen Flessemann-Van Leer, Charlotte von Kirschbaum, James D. Smart, Walter Bryden, John Line, Kazoh Kitamori, K. H. Ting, Hans-Joachim Iwand, John Coleman Bennett, Robert McAfee Brown, and many others.

Chapter 1. Karl Barth:
Christian Theology after Christendom

1. Cited in Ates Orga, *Beethoven* (Illustrated Lives of the Great Composers) (London, New York, Sydney: Omnibus Press, 1983), 161.
2. Karl Barth, *A Karl Barth Reader,* ed. Rolf Joachim Erler and Reiner Marquard, ed. and trans. Geoffrey W. Bromiley (Grand Rapids: Wm. B. Eerdmans Publishing Co., 1986), 113–14. (The segment is from *Letzte Zeugnisse* [Zurich, 1970], 38.)
3. Karl Barth, *Evangelical Theology: An Introduction,* trans. Grover Foley (New York: Holt, Rinehart & Winston, 1963), xiii.
4. Karl Barth, as quoted in Eberhard Busch, *Karl Barth: His Life from Letters and Autobiographical Texts,* trans. John Bowden (London: SCM Press, 1975), 116 (from "Dank und Reverenz," in *Evangelische Theologie,* 1963, 339f.).
5. Karl Barth, *The Humanity of God,* trans. John Newton Thomas and Thomas Wieser (Richmond: John Knox Press, 1960), 13.
6. Ibid., 21.
7. Ibid., 23.
8. Karl Barth, *The Epistle to the Romans,* trans. Edwyn C. Hoskyns from the 6th ed. (London: Oxford University Press, 1933), 10.
9. Ibid., 3.
10. Busch, *Karl Barth,* 115.
11. Barth, *The Epistle to the Romans,* 3 n. 2.
12. Karl Barth, *Zur innern Lage des Christentums* (On the inner situation of Christianity).
13. Edward Thurneysen, cited in *Revolutionary Theology in the Making: Barth-Thurneysen Correspondence, 1914–1925,* trans. James D. Smart (Richmond: John Knox Press, 1964), 21.

14. Ibid., 165.
15. Karl Barth, *The Teaching of the Church Regarding Baptism,* trans. Ernest A. Payne (London: SCM Press, 1948).
16. Ibid., 40.
17. Ibid., 41.
18. Ibid., 42–48.
19. Ibid., 49–52.
20. Ibid., 53.
21. Ibid., 53–54 (italics added).
22. Karl Barth, *Church Dogmatics,* vol. I, part 2, trans. G. T. Thomson and Harold Knight (Edinburgh: T. & T. Clark, 1956).
23. Ibid., 303.
24. Ibid., 333.
25. See Renate Köbler, *In the Shadow of Karl Barth: Charlotte von Kirschbaum,* trans. Keith Crim (Louisville, Ky.: Westminster John Knox Press, 1989), 58ff.
26. Barth, *Church Dogmatics,* I/2, 333.
27. Ibid.
28. Ibid., 334.
29. Ibid.
30. Ibid.
31. Ibid., 335.
32. Ibid.
33. Ibid., 336.
34. Ibid., 337.
35. Ibid., 338.
36. Karl Barth and Johannes Hamel, *How to Serve God in a Marxist Land,* introduction by Robert McAfee Brown, trans. Thomas Wieser (New York: Association Press, 1959), 61–62.
37. Ibid.
38. Ibid., 65.
39. Gary Dorrien, "The 'Postmodern' Barth? The Word of God as True Myth," *Christian Century,* April 2, 1997, 338–42. One can only agree that Barth saw and named the end of modernity; so did all of the other "neo-orthodox" thinkers we are considering here. It is however stretching the point, in my opinion, to suggest that this makes Barth (or any of the others) "postmodern" in any way other than being "after modernity." He certainly did not satisfy himself with fragments and the deconstruction of oppressive systems; he created a system of his own which many, alas, failing to appreciate the courage that it demanded, have found oppressive!

Chapter 2. Paul Tillich:
Systematic Theology—Faith's Quest for Wholeness

1. Wilhelm and Marion Pauck, *Paul Tillich: His Life and Thought,* vol. 1: *Life* (New York: Harper & Row, 1976), 263–64.
2. It seems to me indicative of a shared outlook, as well, that both thinkers had been profoundly moved by Matthias Grünewald's *Crucifixion* and were particularly fond of the book of Ecclesiastes.
3. Both were socialists.
4. George Aichele et al., *The Postmodern Bible* (New Haven, Conn.: Yale University Press, 1995), 10.
5. Dorothee Sölle, *Political Theology,* trans. John Shelley (Philadelphia: Fortress Press, 1971), 23.
6. Douglas Sloan, *Faith and Knowledge* (Louisville, Ky.: Westminster John Knox Press, 1994), 213ff.
7. Wilhelm Pauck, *From Luther to Tillich,* ed. Marion Pauck (San Francisco: Harper & Row, 1984), 163.
8. Ibid.
9. Ibid.
10. Ibid., 164.
11. Paul Tillich, *Systematic Theology,* vol. 1 (Chicago: University of Chicago Press, 1951), xi.
12. Ibid., 148–49 (italics added).
13. See Paul Tillich, *On The Boundary: An Autobiographical Sketch* (New York: Charles Scribner's Sons, 1966).
14. See, for example, Kenneth Hamilton, *The System and the Gospel: A Critique of Paul Tillich* (Grand Rapids: Wm. B. Eerdmans Publishing Co., 1967).
15. Charles W. Kegley and Robert W. Bretall, eds., *The Theology of Paul Tillich* (New York: Macmillan Publishing Co., 1952), x.
16. Ibid., 329–30 (italics added).
17. Paul Tillich, *Biblical Religion and the Search for Ultimate Reality* (Chicago: University of Chicago Press, 1955).
18. Ibid., 11.
19. Tillich, *Systematic Theology,* 1:3.
20. Douglas John Hall, *Thinking the Faith: Christian Theology in a North American Context,* vol. 1 (Minneapolis: Fortress Press, 1991), 360f.
21. Tillich, *Systematic Theology,* 2:13.
22. Ibid., 2:15 (italics added).
23. Martin Luther, *Werke* (Weimar, 1883–), 5.163.28.

24. Paul Tillich, *Dynamics of Faith* (New York: Harper & Brothers, 1957), 16ff.

Chapter 3. Reinhold Niebuhr:
An American Theology of the Tragic—and Beyond

1. See W. Pauck, *From Luther to Tillich,* 191: In his first major book, published in 1923, Tillich "spoke eloquently of the 'courage to truth' (*Mut zur Wahrheit*). The warmth and urgency of his words gave the impression that he himself was existentially involved in this."
2. Rolf Hochhuth, *Soldiers: An Obituary for Geneva,* trans. Robert David MacDonald (New York: Grove Press, 1968), 56.
3. Robert Langbaum, *The Gayety of Vision: A Study of Isak Dinesen's Art* (New York: Random House, 1965), 125.
4. See Sydney E. Ahlstrom, *A Religious History of the American People,* vol. 1 (Garden City, N.Y.: Doubleday & Co. (Image Books), 1975), 34.
5. See Reinhold Niebuhr, "Epilogue: A View of Life from the Sidelines," in *The Essential Reinhold Niebuhr: Selected Essays and Addresses,* ed. Robert McAfee Brown (New Haven, Conn., and London: Yale University Press, 1986), 251.
6. Theological Declaration of Barmen, II.2. From Arthur C. Cochrane, *The Church's Confession under Hitler* (Philadelphia: Westminster Press, 1962), 239.
7. Brown, *Essential Reinhold Niebuhr,* 13.
8. Ibid.
9. Douglas John Hall, *Lighten Our Darkness: Toward an Indigenous Theology of the Cross* (Philadelphia: Westminster Press, 1976).
10. Brown, *Essential Reinhold Niebuhr,* 16–17 (italics added).
11. Reinhold Niebuhr, *Beyond Tragedy* (New York: Charles Scribner's Sons, 1937, 1965).
12. Ibid., [xii].
13. These included John Bennett, Cyril Richardson, and Joseph Haroutunian—but not one who was often his critic, his brother Helmut Richard, who wrote to him, "These sermons have your authentic ring in them. Of course I get them better than your critics because I remain more a preacher than anything else, despite the fact that I preach little. There is more positive assurance, more faith, more hope and love in this book than in anything I've seen in a long time. Your Gifford lectures will be more recondite but can't be deeper." Richard Fox, *Reinhold*

Niebuhr: A Biography (New York: Pantheon Books, 1985), 183–84. See Fox's extended discussion of the appearance of this book, of which he says, "More than any of his other books, *Beyond Tragedy* captures the play of [Niebuhr's] mind: unsystematic, restless, eruptive. It also reveals the character of his faith: acquainted with suffering and absurdity, yet built on an ultimate trust in the meaningfulness of life and the goodness of God" (pp. 181f.).

14. R. Niebuhr, *Beyond Tragedy*, x–xi.
15. Gary A. Gaudin and Douglas John Hall, eds., *Reinhold Niebuhr (1892–1971): A Centenary Appraisal,* McGill Studies in Religion, vol. 3 (Atlanta: Scholars Press, 1994), 127–42.
16. Ibid.
17. See Tillich's essay, "Reinhold Niebuhr's Doctrine of Knowledge," in *Reinhold Niebuhr: His Religious, Social, and Political Thought,* ed. Charles W. Kegley and Robert W. Bretall (New York: Macmillan Publishing Co., 1956), 42. I am of the opinion that Niebuhr's criticism of "Greek" thought was in fact a criticism of Aristotelian thought, primarily, with some aspects of Plato in the background. He did not, I believe, distinguish sufficiently between Hellenic and Hellenistic traditions, and he had more in common with Socrates and the pre-Socratics than he appears to have thought. Like many of us who are Protestants and educated in North America chiefly, Niebuhr's educational background was limited in the realms both of history and philosophy. Nevertheless, I believe that he was right to intuit a serious and unbridgeable gulf between the relational ontology (my word, not his!) of Jerusalem and the substantialistic ontologies of much (though not all) of Athens.
18. R. Niebuhr, *Beyond Tragedy,* 165.
19. Ibid., 19.
20. Ibid.
21. See the essay of the German theologian and pastor Friedrich Hufendiek, entitled "Germany: A Difficult Fatherland," in Gaudin and Hall, *Reinhold Niebuhr,* 29ff.
22. R. Niebuhr, *Leaves from the Notebook of a Tamed Cynic* (Louisville, Ky.: Westminster John Knox Press, 1990), 70.
23. "Der Theologe der Gottes unverborgene Herrlichkeit sucht, nennt das Übel gut und Gutes übel; der Theologe des Kreuzes nennt die Dinge beim rechten Namen." (The theologian of glory calls evil good and good evil. The theologian of the cross calls the thing what it actually is.) (*Luther's Works,* vol. 31 [Philadelphia: Fortress Press, 1957], 40–41.)

24. R. Niebuhr, *Beyond Tragedy,* 20.
25. Jean Martin Charcot (1825–1893), quoted in D. M. Thomas, *The White Hotel* (Harmondsworth, Middlesex: Penguin Books, 1981), 111.
26. Nathaniel Hawthorne, *The House of the Seven Gables* (Signet Classic), 42.
27. R. Niebuhr, *Beyond Tragedy,* 20.
28. Paul Tillich, *The World Situation,* Social Ethics Series 2 (Philadelphia: Fortress Press, 1965), 49.

Chapter 4. Dietrich Bonhoeffer:
Discipleship as World Commitment

1. Dietrich Bonhoeffer, *The Cost of Discipleship,* trans. R. H. Fuller (London: SCM Press, 1948).
2. I have tried to characterize that "moral rectitude" in my *Why Christian? For Those on the Edges of Faith* (Minneapolis: Fortress Press, 1998).
3. Bonhoeffer, *Cost of Discipleship,* 37.
4. John A. T. Robinson, *Honest to God* (London: SCM Press, 1963).
5. Ibid., quoted from the jacket of the sixth impression, 1963.
6. Ibid., 85 n. 1.
7. Dietrich Bonhoeffer, *Letters and Papers from Prison* (enlarged ed.), ed. Eberhard Bethge, trans. Reginald Fuller, Frank Clarke, et al. (New York: Macmillan Publishing Co., 1953), 360–61.
8. Larry Rasmussen, with Renate Bethge, *Dietrich Bonhoeffer—His Significance for North Americans* (Minneapolis: Fortress Press, 1990), 144–73 ("An Ethic of the Cross").
9. Quoted by John de Gruchy, *Dietrich Bonhoeffer: Witness to Jesus Christ* (London: Collins, 1987), 216 (italics added).
10. Dietrich Bonhoeffer, *Ethics,* ed. Eberhard Bethge, trans. Neville Horton Smith (London: SCM Press, 1955).
11. Ibid., 56.
12. Ibid., 57.
13. Ibid., 142 (italics added).
14. Bonhoeffer, *Letters and Papers,* 369–70.

Chapter 5. Emil Brunner:
Truth as Meeting

1. I. John Hesselink, "Emil Brunner: A Centennial Perspective," *Christian Century,* December 13, 1989: 1171f.

2. Brunner not only taught languages at the University of Leeds (1913–1914) but he studied for a year (1919–1920) at Union Theological Seminary in New York and was Visiting Professor at Princeton Theological Seminary throughout another momentous year, 1938–1939.

Indeed, it is somewhat ironic that the linkage of Brunner's name with that of Barth in Anglo-Saxon lands is due in part to Brunner's linguistic advantage. He himself writes: "To them [English-speaking readers] I became known first of all under a double name: Barth and Brunner. Since Karl Barth himself did not speak English at the time and therefore went neither to England nor to America, I was regarded more or less as the English mouthpiece of this Barth-Brunner theology, until suddenly the well-known controversy over natural theology made it evident that Barth and Brunner were not identical twins." In Brunner's response to Wilhelm Pauck's essay in Charles W. Kegley, ed., *The Theology of Emil Brunner*, Library of Living Theology 3 (New York: Macmillan Publishing Co., 1962), 328.

3. Charles Kegley, in his introduction to Brunner in vol. 3 of the Library of Living Theology series, writes: "Brunner's total work is characterized by a balance and judiciousness which, if the phrase did not now have undesirable connotations, could best be described as 'the middle way.' Thus, Brunner's interpretation of Christianity is free from the extremes of the right, the early neo-orthodox and supernaturalist's denial of natural theology and the like, and of the left, the radical empiricist denial that we may achieve anything knowledgeable and/or significant unless it grows out of and can be tested and confirmed by experience." Kegley, *Theology of Emil Brunner*, xi–xii.

4. Emil Brunner, *The Divine-Human Encounter* (London: SCM Press, 1944).

5. Brunner himself commented on this failure in his "Intellectual Autobiography" for the Kegley volume: "Unfortunately, the English title, *The Divine-Human Encounter*, doesn't succeed in expressing the fundamental thought of the book, namely, that which is specific about the Christian understanding of truth. Here I placed the biblical understanding over and against the Greek understanding which is the foundation of our Western philosophy and science." In Kegley, *Theology of Emil Brunner*, 12.

Brunner is even more outspoken in his rejection of the 1944 English title in the preface to the 1964 revision, in which he actually accuses both the translator and the publisher of the earlier edition of "caprice" in their choice of a title, and whimsically remarks that the success of the book permits him, nevertheless, to offer the publisher "retrospectively the absolution for which he had never asked."

6. The original translation by Loos was retained, and new and revised material was prepared by David Cairns in consultation with T. H. L. Parker.

7. It also connects more directly with the theme of one of the sources from which Brunner learned this language—Martin Buber's *Ich und Du*: "All real living is meeting." (*I and Thou*, trans. Ronald Gregor Smith [Edinburgh: T. & T. Clark, 1937], 11. The German original appeared in 1923.)

8. Kegley, *Theology of Emil Brunner*, 12.

9. Ibid., 16.

10. Hesselink, "Emil Brunner," 1172.

11. Karl Barth, *The Doctrine of the Word of God (Prolegomena to Church Dogmatics, Being Vol. I, Part I)*, trans. G. T. Thomson (New York: Charles Scribner's Sons, 1936), 22.

12. Kegley, *Theology of Emil Brunner*, 11.

13. In an interesting excursus in the third and final volume of his *Dogmatics*, Brunner expresses his immense appreciation for Buber's famous *I and Thou* while at the same time distancing himself from the great Jewish thinker's "teaching on the Apostles' misunderstanding of faith" in *Two Types of Faith*. "[T]hrough his teaching about the two dimensions I/Thou, I/It, [Buber] has performed . . . a tremendous service to theology, which Karl Heim was the first to appreciate as a 'Copernican Revolution.'" *Two Types of Faith,* however, in which Buber distinguished faith as understood by the Hebrew Bible *and Jesus* from the apostolic theology of Paul and John, Brunner considered "a major attack upon Christianity" without intending to be so. He acknowledged, however, that the attack is justified in many ways because "the Christian Church has itself given him occasion for this misunderstanding"—namely, by failing to differentiate between the objectification of truth in doctrine and the biblical conception of truth as meeting. *The Christian Doctrine of the Church, Faith, and the Consummation, Dogmatics,* vol. 3, trans. David Cairns in collaboration with T. H. L. Parker (London: Lutterworth Press, 1962).

14. Ibid. Brunner's sense of indebtedness to Kierkegaard is further illustrated by the inclusion, in the revised edition of *Truth as*

Encounter, of four new introductory chapters in which Kierkegaard is frequently cited and functions, indeed, as the key figure in Brunner's fascinating survey of the evolution of philosophical, theological, and scientific thought.

15. For purposes of quotation, I shall use the original (1944) English edition rather than the revised and enlarged edition of 1963. I do so for two reasons: first, the text of the earlier edition, though for the most part retained in the later, has a directness that is somewhat muted by the format of the 1963 edition; second, while the new "Part I" is illuminating in its own right, the essential argument is the same in both editions, and it helps *us* to gain historical-theological perspective if we realize how early in our own century this approach to theological truth was being advocated.
16. Brunner, *Divine-Human Encounter,* 195.
17. Ibid., 17.
18. Ibid., 18.
19. Ibid., 19.
20. Ibid., 19–20.
21. Ibid.
22. Ibid., 22.
23. Ibid., 25.
24. Ibid., 26.
25. Ibid., 27.
26. Ibid., 27–28.
27. That is perhaps what H. Richard Niebuhr tends to offer.
28. Ibid., 121f.
29. Ibid., 122.
30. Ibid., 14.
31. Ibid., 31–32 (italics added).
32. Ibid., 53f.
33. Ibid., 59.
34. Ibid.
35. Ibid., 60–61.
36. Ibid., 61.
37. Ibid., 74.
38. Ibid., 86.
39. Ibid.
40. Ibid., 112.
41. The final sentences of the book. Ibid., 147 (p. 198 in the revised edition).

Chapter 6. H. Richard Niebuhr:
Christ and (Post-Christian) Culture

1. See Hans W. Frei, "H. Richard Niebuhr on History, Church and Nation," in *The Legacy of H. Richard Niebuhr,* ed. Ronald F. Thiemann (Minneapolis: Fortress Press, 1991), 9–11. See also Douglas F. Ottati, "God and Ourselves: The Witness of H. Richard Niebuhr," in *Christian Century,* April 2, 1997, 346.
2. H. Richard Niebuhr, "An Attempt at a Theological Analysis of Missionary Motivation," N.Y.C. Missionary Research Library Occasional Bulletin 15, no. 1 (January 1963): 1f.
3. John Godsey, *The Promise of H. Richard Niebuhr* (Philadelphia and New York: J. B. Lippincott Co., 1970), 38.
4. H. Richard Niebuhr, "Reformation: Continuing Imperative," in *Christian Century,* March 2, 1960, 249.
5. Godsey, *Promise,* 99–100.
6. Frei, "H. Richard Niebuhr," 9.
7. "Niebuhr . . . faced the challenge that relativism poses for the theological task. He did not search for some Archimedean point outside the web of history. Instead he acknowledged the historicity of Christian theology. He recognized the finitude of all human knowledge. He insisted on the relational nature of religious knowledge. He used the term 'confessional' in his early work to express this relational nature of faith and theology. Theology is historically and socially conditioned, as all human knowledge is. Theology, moreover, reflects the relational nature of religious valuations. Therefore, theology should criticize any absolutization of finite social, cultural, national values, including theological notions and religious values." Francis Schüssler Fiorenza, "Theology as Responsible Valuation or Reflective Equilibrium," in Thiemann, *Legacy,* 35–36.
8. H. Richard Niebuhr, *The Meaning of Revelation* (New York: Macmillan Publishing Co., 1941), 176–77.
9. Thiemann, *Legacy,* 81.
10. Interestingly enough, as we shall note presently, Suzanne de Diétrich, who spent most of her life among university students, felt that the first step in any kind of evangelical work and Christian study should be the apparently simple but profoundly demanding task of acquainting people with the life of Jesus as testified to in the scriptures.
11. H. Richard Niebuhr, *Christ and Culture* (New York: Harper & Brothers, 1951), 11. Unless otherwise indicated, the quotations that

follow will all come from the section of *Christ and Culture* entitled, "Towards a Definition of Christ," 11–29.

12. Ibid., 29. The ideas and language throughout this thumbnail sketch are remarkably reminiscent of my own discussion of Christology in the third volume of my trilogy—though at the time I did not have the work of H. R. Niebuhr at all in mind, and had indeed never really appropriated it. It is obvious that what we have had in common in our endeavors to articulate a credible picture of the Christ is, negatively speaking, a strong sense of the remoteness and incommunicability of the metaphysical concepts of conventional Christology and, positively speaking, a new appreciation for the relational, narrative, and historical approach of Hebraic-Christian faith to all theological questions, including that of trinitarian theology. See *Professing the Faith: Christian Theology in a North American Context* (Minneapolis: Fortress Press, 1996), part 3, 363–548.

Chapter 7. Suzanne de Diétrich:
The Word of God for the People of God

1. Hans-Ruedi Weber, *The Courage to Live: A Biography of Suzanne de Diétrich* (Geneva: WCC Publications, 1995), 130.
2. See Renate Köbler, *In the Shadow of Karl Barth,* trans. Keith Crim (Louisville, Ky.: Westminster John Knox Press, 1989).
3. Weber, *Courage,* 31.
4. Ibid., 124. De Diétrich frequently refers to the experience of women in her writings, and a recurring theme is the manner in which Christianity—in its *biblical* expression, at least—assumes a radical equality of women and men; specifically, in which *Jesus* is the "liberator" of woman. "By this whole attitude towards women Jesus has wrought a silent revolution. . . . We see women at the foot of the Cross. And it was to them that it pleased the Lord to make known the first news of the Resurrection. From that time forward woman was to have her place in the Church of Christ alongside of man, the recipient of the same grace, of the same salvation." Suzanne de Diétrich, *Free Men: Meditations on the Bible Today,* trans. Olive Wyon (London: SCM Press, 1961), 80–81.
5. Weber, *Courage,* 21.
6. Ibid., 31.
7. Quoted in ibid., 63–64.
8. Among these, I am particularly indebted to Marie-Jeanne de Haller

Coleman, who was her associate and friend. I am also grateful to a former student, Ms. Tamsin Jones, for her research in this subject.

9. Weber, *Courage,* 19.

10. Ibid., 19.

11. Ibid., 56.

12. Ibid., 37.

13. In saying this, I do not wish to belittle important work that is undertaken *today* within the S.C.M. and the W.S.C.F. It seems quite clear to me, however, that the 1960s, with their odd but heady admixture of dionysian utopianism and cultural cynicism, deeply affected the spirit of the Christian student movement; and this is nowhere more conspicuous than in the loss of serious study, within the context of the modern university, of the Judeo-Christian texts and traditions as the Christian community's entrée to historical responsibility. After 1960, that focus was replaced by an allegedly more immediate and activist involvement in social developments, causes, and issues. (De Dićtrich herself lamented this loss [see Weber, *Courage,* 139.]) In short, what happened to the intellectual cutting edge of mainstream Protestantism at large in the second half of the century, a matter which I shall take up presently in my Conclusions, happened earlier and rather more dramatically to the S.C.M., namely, an effective shift from struggling with the christological center named by de Diétrich in the earlier quotation to diverse ethical and cultural concerns. The importance of these concerns cannot be doubted, but they are concerns that require a foundation in a thinking faith if Christians are to address them wisely. Without such a foundation, ethical concerns divide more consistently than they unite the Christian community or equip it for common worldly witness.

14. Weber, *Courage,* 12.

15. Ibid., 19.

16. Ibid., 13.

17. Ibid.

18. Suzanne de Diétrich, *Discovering the Bible: A Practical Handbook for Bible Study* (Coonoor, Nilgiris [India]: The Youth Departments of the World Council of Churches and the World Council of Christian Education and Sunday School Association, 1952), 19–20 (italics added).

19. Ibid., 20.

20. Ibid.

21. Ibid., 23.

22. Ibid., 21.

23. Ibid., 39.
24. Lucien Gautier, biblical professor at Geneva, "full of admiration for [her] tremendous work and great erudition," offered to teach her the two languages, which he felt that she could sufficiently master in a few months. Weber, *Courage*, 57.
25. Ibid.
26. Jacques Ellul, *The Presence of the Kingdom*, trans. Olive Wyon (London: SCM Press, 1948), 37.
27. Masao Takenaka, *God Is Rice: Asian Culture and Christian Faith* (Geneva: World Council of Churches, 1986), 10–11.
28. De Diétrich, *Discovering the Bible*, 24.
29. Ibid., 51.
30. Ibid., 52.
31. *The Bible Speaks to You* is the title of one of Robert McAfee Brown's own early books (Philadelphia: Westminster Press, 1955).
32. Another example: Commenting on Abraham's journey to Mount Moriah to obey God's command that he sacrifice Isaac, his son [Genesis 22], she writes: "The story of these three days of the journey of the father and the child towards Mount Moriah are some of the most harrowing pages in the whole of the Bible. They foreshadow another three days' journey, when the Son 'set his face to go to Jerusalem' (Luke 13:31–33)."
33. De Diétrich, *Free Men*, 23.
34. Ibid., 79.
35. Weber, *Courage*, 86.
36. "There is a problem with being well off; and all my life it has remained insoluble. What does it mean to be poor. I can never be quite at ease when I read certain passages of the gospel. I always ask myself what it means to go to the limits set by the gospel. I do not know." De Diétrich, quoted in Weber, *Courage*, 86.
37. De Diétrich, *Free Men*, 100–101.
38. Weber, *Courage*, 152.
39. From a paper presented in 1937 at the second ecumenical retreat, titled "The Bible and Ecumenism," quoted in Weber, *Courage*, 79.
40. De Diétrich, *Discovering the Bible*, 35.
41. Ibid., 35–36.
42. Weber, *Courage*, 142.

Conclusions

1. Wilhelm Pauck, in Kegley and Bretall, *Theology of Emil Brunner*.
2. Ibid., 34.

3. Ibid.

4. Ibid., 35.

5. Ibid.

6. Ibid. Interestingly, Pauck claims that the "most radical and incisive spokesman" for this point of view "is Rudolf Bultmann, who, unfortunately, was misunderstood by many when he introduced the term 'demythologizing' in order to make plain in what way the Bible must be translated as to both form and content in order that it may be understood by the man of today. Bultmann does not discard what he considers the archaic mythological worldview of the Bible. He stresses again and again that the men of the Bible presuppose this worldview. Yet he says that because we no longer think in the same mythical terms as the men of the Bible, we must demythologize the Bible . . . *so that it can be comprehended*" (italics added).

7. Ibid., 36–37.

8. "There are large passages in Barth's *Dogmatics* which are nothing other than reverberations of Luther's faith. Brunner calls upon Luther again and again as his chief ally, especially insofar as he understands the Christian faith and life as a personal encounter with the gospel of the forgiveness of sin. Bultmann's existentialism is Lutheran through and through. Niebuhr's basic teaching is nothing but a modern version of Luther's view of men as *simul justus et peccator*. And it is characteristic even of Tillich that the most powerful and persuasive passages of his book *The Courage to Be* are directly inspired by Martin Luther." Ibid., 37.

9. Ibid., 38 (italics added).

10. Ibid., 35.

11. Ibid.

12. Notably in Douglas John Hall, *Lighten Our Darkness: Toward an Indigenous Theology of the Cross* (Philadelphia: Westminster Press, 1976), *God and Human Suffering: An Exercise in the Theology of the Cross* (Minneapolis: Augsburg Fortress Press, 1986), and the trilogy subtitled *Christian Theology in a North American Context* (vol. 1, *Thinking the Faith,* 1991; vol. 2, *Professing the Faith,* 1996; vol. 3, *Confessing the Faith,* 1997 (Minneapolis: Fortress Press).

13. Jürgen Moltmann, *The Crucified God: The Cross of Christ as the Foundation and Criticism of Christian Theology,* trans. R. W. Wilson and John Bowden (London: SCM Press, 1973), 72.

14. Paul Tillich, *The Courage to Be* (New Haven, Conn., and London: Yale University Press, 1952), 188.

15. See in this connection Walter Brueggemann's monumental new work, *Theology of the Old Testament* (Minneapolis: Fortress Press, 1997), especially the introductory chapters, where the author notes, among other things, that "historical criticism," that grand and in many ways admirable and necessary attempt at objectivity in biblical studies, "as it has come to be practiced *has been notorious for its lack of interest in the actual expression of the text itself*" (p. 53; italics added).

16. Jean Bethke Elshtain, *Democracy on Trial* (Toronto: House of Anansi, 1993), 3.

17. Ibid., 75.

18. Ibid., 8.

19. Ibid., 75–76. The quotation is from Sheldon Wolin, "Democracy, Difference and Recognition," *Political Theory* 21 (August 1993): 468.

20. I am quoting here from the transcript of an extensive CBC radio interview with Professor Todd Gitlin, "Todd Gitlin in Conversation," Toronto: Canadian Broadcasting Corporation, 1997.

21. *McLean's* 110, no. 50 (December 15, 1997): 40–47.

22. I am writing this in the wake of President Clinton's State of the Union address on January 27, 1998, and my point is almost tragically demonstrated by the terrible contrast between the theatrical show of confidence in the tone of that address and the reality of public scandal, suspicion, and hypocrisy that so intruded itself into the pageantry and rhetoric of the occasion that it colored every word and gesture of the speaker.

23. "Theologus gloriae dicit malum bonum et bonum malum. Theologus crucis dicit id res est." The language of this thesis was suggested to Luther by Isaiah 5:20: "Woe to those who call evil good and good evil, who put darkness for light and light for darkness, who put bitter for sweet and sweet for bitter!"

24. William Hordern made this point in his still-useful 1955 book *A Layman's Guide to Protestant Theology* (New York: Macmillan Publishing Co.): "Despite its paradoxical flavor, the term [neo-orthodoxy] is a good description. The essence of the movement has been a return to orthodoxy, but it is orthodoxy with a difference. It is a position which is held usually by former liberals and it is deeply colored by the fact that its representatives were liberals. This coloring may be discerned in two ways. On the one hand, certain aspects of liberal thought are found in the new movement. Fundamentalism is repudiated as savagely by the neo-orthodox as it is by the liberal. Biblical criticism is

accepted in its most radical forms. But the fact that the neo-orthodox are converted liberals is also found in the extreme reaction against certain liberal concepts, such as the use of reason or natural theology" (p. 122).

Index of Names